CANES VS. GATORS

INSIDE THE LEGENDARY MIAMI HURRICANES AND FLORIDA GATORS FOOTBALL RIVALRY

MARTY STRASEN

Foreword by BROCK BERLIN

SPORTS PUBLISHING

Sports Publishing books may be purchased in bulk at special discounts for sales promotion, corporate gifts, fund-raising, or educational purposes. Special editions can also be created to specifications. For details, contact the Special Sales Department, Sports Publishing, 307 West 36th Street, 11th Floor, New York, NY 10018 or sportspubbooks@skyhorsepublishing.com.

Sports Publishing® is a registered trademark of Skyhorse Publishing, Inc.®, a Delaware corporation.

Visit our website at www.sportspubbooks.com.

10 9 8 7 6 5 4 3 2 1

Library of Congress Cataloging-in-Publication Data is available on file.

Cover design by Tom Lau
Cover photo: AP Images

ISBN: 978-1-61321-806-8
Ebook ISBN: 978-1-61321-834-1

Printed in the United States of America

TABLE OF CONTENTS

FOREWORD

MY FOOTBALL CAREER was filled with crazy coincidences. My first collegiate start, in my final game as a member of the Florida Gators, was at the BCS Orange Bowl game in Miami on January 2, 2002. I had already made a big decision to transfer from Florida to the University of Miami, but it was not common knowledge at the time. So there I was, in my future hometown, wearing Gator orange and blue for one last time in a win over Maryland. After sitting out one year because of the transfer, my next game in this same town would be my first home game as the starting quarterback for the Miami Hurricanes. Sure enough, it came against my old Florida teammates in 2003. And then, in what might have been the craziest coincidence of all, my last college game took place in the 2004 Peach Bowl against—you guessed it—the Florida Gators.

CANES VS. GATORS

I am a Cane, through and through. Though I started my career at Florida, learned a lot from Coach Spurrier, and remember my first time running onto the field in The Swamp like it was yesterday, I bleed orange and green. I am proud to call myself a Cane. My greatest college memory, hands down, was that first game against the Gators in 2003. Coming back from 33–10 down in the third quarter to when it looked like everything that could possibly go wrong was going wrong. Winning that game started it all for me at Miami, and I wouldn't trade my time in Coral Gables for anything in the world.

Rivalries like Florida-Miami are what college football is all about. There's so much pride, so much passion. You want to win those games more than any other game you play. For the players who grew up in Florida, it's about bragging rights against guys you played high school football against and have known your whole life. For me, being from Louisiana, it was about big-time college football and getting to be part of something with so much tradition and years of history.

My first experience with the rivalry was in the 2001 Sugar Bowl, after the 2000 season. I was a true freshman at Florida and man, what an atmosphere. There must have been sixty guys from both teams on Bourbon Street a few nights before the game. It's hard to put into words the fight that took place that night in the street. I remember running up on the scene after hearing what was about to take place and could not believe what was going on. There must have been at least thirty seconds of fighting with a lot of big strong guys in there before the police came in and broke it up. That's a long time for a fight like that. You can read more about the fight and the game later in this book.

That was my introduction to the rivalry and the point where I really saw the intensity of feelings—the hatred—between Florida and Miami. My college football career connected me to both schools in a very unique way.

I wanted a chance to play, but as a true sophomore at Florida I found myself behind a great quarterback, Rex Grossman, who was a redshirt sophomore. I thought about waiting my turn by redshirting and coming back the next year to compete for the position. I really just wanted to play. Coach Spurrier was very supportive when I asked for my release. Larry Coker, the coach at Miami, had recruited me out of high school so there was a comfort level there. Transferring to the University of Miami seemed like the best opportunity for me. I knew I would be sitting out a year, but during that time I would be able to learn from Ken Dorsey, who was coming back for his senior season with the Canes.

Once I was eligible to play and earned the starting position in 2003, it was an amazing feeling. My very first game was at Louisiana Tech in my hometown of Shreveport. The only thing that could top playing in the town I grew up in was, as I mentioned earlier, playing my first home game against the Florida Gators. You truly can't dream up scenarios like that.

I'm still good friends today with some of the teammates I had while in Gainesville. Gator Nation is so big and the fans are so passionate. Coming to Miami, which is obviously a much smaller school, it was like joining a fraternity. There's a brotherhood of guys who have worn "The U" on their helmets. You really understand that you're not just playing for your team, your coaches, your teammates, and the fans. You're playing for everyone who's ever played for the Canes, and upholding that great legacy. It's incredible how the alumni come back and reach out to you, and how invested they are in the program. I am forever indebted to guys like Bernie Kosar, Steve Walsh, Gino Torretta, and Ken Dorsey for the time they invested and wisdom they imparted in my life.

Gainesville and Miami are really night-and-day different. Florida is a big school in a small town, where everyone is crazy about the Gators. Miami is a small school in a huge town where there is always something going on. It's such a different feel. It's also one of the many things that make this rivalry so great.

I understand that there are politics and conference scheduling issues that have contributed to Florida and Miami no longer playing every year. In my opinion, discontinuing this great rivalry was a huge loss for college football. I'm glad these teams will be on the same field again in 2019, and I'm hopeful they will figure out how to get them playing each other regularly again. This rivalry is too great, too special and has too much tradition. It's just a great game for college football fans.

Fans want to see Miami play Florida. I want to see Miami play Florida. My hope is that, as you read this book, you remember the intense feelings and great pride that are on the line every time the Hurricanes and Gators line up across from each other. No matter which school you support, here's hoping that can once again become a regular occurrence!

Brock Berlin

BROCK BERLIN HOLDS *a distinct place in the Florida-Miami rivalry. He quarterbacked both schools, starting his career with the Gators before transferring and finishing it as a two-year starter for the Hurricanes. He also engineered one of the biggest wins in the history of the series, rallying Miami from a 33–10 deficit to a 38–33 victory over his former school at the Orange Bowl in 2003. His Canes scored 28 unanswered points in the last 18 1/2 minutes of that game.*

In two years at Miami, Brock threw for more than 5,000 yards and 34 touchdowns. He defeated Florida twice and Florida State three times, without a loss to either school while at UM. He played briefly in the NFL, starting a game for the Rams in 2007. Brock now works in medical sales in his hometown of Shreveport, Louisiana, where lives with his wife, Amy, and their three children.

CANES VS. GATORS

Brock Berlin holds an exclusive place in the history of the Miami-Florida football rivalry, having started at quarterback for both schools. In his first game against his former school after transferring to Miami, he directed the Hurricanes to 28 unanswered points for an unforgettable win over the Gators in 2003. *AP Photo/Tony Gutierrez (left) and David J. Phillip (right)*

INTRODUCTION: SUNSHINE STATE HATE

THIS IS THE story of an unusual canoe trip.

When the University of Florida and the University of Miami began playing football games against each other in 1938, the canoe used for this journey was not a canoe at all. Rather, she was a majestic, almost-two-hundred-year-old cypress tree with no intention of getting wet. A well-placed lightning strike changed that, however, and in 1955 the city of Hollywood, Florida, donated a six-foot canoe to serve as a trophy for the winner of the then-annual contest between the Gators and Hurricanes. The Seminole War Canoe was traded proudly, and fiercely, between the schools for decades before falling on hard times, being rescued from a trash heap and docked, finally, in the UM Sports Hall of Fame in 1989.

Florida fans believe she should be sent to Gainesville. Miami fans might love for her to spring free from her landing place and once again be awarded to the winner of a rivalry game that is no longer a regular on the college football docket. And anyone familiar with the history between UF and UM can probably agree on this: her donors should have chosen a sturdier vessel than a wooden canoe to navigate the turbulent waters of this rivalry.

Florida and Miami no longer play each other on a regular basis. It was a UF decision that further fueled the fire in the series. When they did, this was one of the most heated rivalries in sports.

"Hatred," said longtime *Gainesville Sun* writer Pat Dooley, who has covered Florida sports for decades, when asked what the UF-UM rivalry brings to mind. "I think that it was the most vile, vicious series. You know, Florida fans and Florida State fans don't get along. Florida and Georgia don't get along. But Florida and Miami *hate* each other."

Joe Zagacki, veteran radio voice of the Hurricanes, agrees wholeheartedly.

"I'm born and raised in Miami, so I was raised to hate the Gators," Zagacki explained. "Then my daughter decided to attend the University of Florida. And people were like, 'What the hell?' They have a great university, a respected university, a very tough university to get into at the University of Florida. So that's my disclosure on that. I thought I would hate them a little bit less, but I don't. I hate them just as much."

The rivalry is the oldest among the "power" schools that make Florida one of the elite national hotbeds of college football. The Gators and Hurricanes first played in 1938, with Miami posting a surprising 19–7 win in Gainesville on October 15. "Miami's Brilliant Comeback Beats Florida" and "Hurricane Hits Gainesville" screamed the newspaper headlines the following morning.[1]

Miami took the win as confirmation that it had reached the big time. And, in fact, the Hurricanes went on to enjoy perhaps their best season to that point, suffering just two losses in 10 games. If any of the three-thousand-plus UM supporters on hand in Gainesville that day thought the Hurricanes had surpassed the Gators for state supremacy, however, they were mistaken. Florida beat Miami in each of the next three seasons, by a combined score of 73–6. Since then, in addition to being one of the most intense rivalries in college football, it has been one of the closest. Miami leads the all-time series 29–26.

"There are some rivalries that really aren't rivalries because they're so one-sided," said Urban Meyer, who coached Florida to national championships in 2006 and '08. "It's a rivalry when you've got two good teams, and there's some semblance of balance. It's not one-sided. So I think this is a great rivalry . . . great players on both sides and great, passionate fan bases."

---

[1]George Walsh, "Hurricane Hits Gainesville," University of Miami football yearbook, 1939.

The Hurricanes held a 9–7 series advantage when the canoe floated into the rivalry before the 1955 game. From the day of their first game in 1938, the schools squared off every year with one exception—a '43 hiatus due to World War II—through 1987. For most of those years, the game carried no significant national implications. Neither team soared to prominence until much later. To fans of each school, however, it was a day to circle on the calendar.

"I remember being a kid and taking great rejoice when the Gators, I think, were winless," said Zagacki, referring to Florida's forgettable 0–10–1 season in 1979. "They came into the Orange Bowl for the last game of the year and Miami [beat] them. I thought this was the greatest day of my life."

Over the years, both schools also developed a heated rivalry with Florida State University. In fact, largely because Florida and Miami no longer battle on a regular basis, most fans from both schools consider the game against FSU their greatest in-state rivalry.

That does not dilute the venom between the Gators and the Hurricanes when the schools do get together—or even when the topic arises in conversation around bars, beaches, or other gatherings in the Sunshine State. Most agree that the mention of Florida does more to rile Miami fans than the mention of the Hurricanes does in Gainesville.

"I think the rivalry was more us than it was them, because they were the University of Florida and we were the University of Miami," former Hurricanes head coach Larry Coker said.

"They thought they were the big brother and we were the little brother. That's how our players looked at it, and they didn't like that very much."

"It's natural for Miami to really sort of dislike Florida," added Steve Spurrier, who coached the Gators to their first consensus national title in 1996 and faced the Hurricanes as a UF player as well. "Florida's the big, rich school now. Of course our [Florida] tradition wasn't all that super in the '70s and '80s. If you're a smaller private school, which Miami is . . . you just don't like the big school. You don't like the big wealthy school, and that's what Florida is."

The Hurricanes' dislike of the Gators reached new heights in 1971 thanks to an incident known as the "Gator Flop." UF quarterback John Reaves was one good completion shy of the NCAA record for career passing yards in his final game, but Miami had the ball and the clock was about to expire in a game the Gators led by a 45–8 score. Florida coach Doug Dickey, with some nudging from his players, instructed his defense to fall to the ground and let the Hurricanes score so Reaves would get another chance to break the mark. They did. And minutes later, Reaves did it. The ramifications live to this day.

"The flop was the most embarrassing thing that happened to Miami in their history," said former Hurricanes coach Howard Schnellenberger.

It was just one example of boiling blood between players, coaches, students, and fans of these schools, separated by about five hours by car. There was the 1966 Miami upset of Florida after which Hurricanes coach Walt Kichefski raved about the taste of Gator meat. There was the 1980 game in Gainesville when UF fans pelted the visitors from Miami with tangerines and oranges, prompting Schnellenberger to run up the score with an unnecessary late field goal.

There was brawling on Bourbon Street before the 2001 Sugar Bowl in which Spurrier coached for the only time against Miami, and three seasons later there was UM quarterback Brock Berlin, a UF transfer, doing the "Gator chomp" with his arms after directing a furious comeback to beat his former school.

"When you play a team over and over and over again, somewhere along the way somebody's going to get mad," offered Mark Richt, a former Miami quarterback who returned to his alma mater as head coach beginning in 2016. "Somewhere along the way somebody's going to get their feelings hurt. Somewhere along the way tension is going to be building up over time, and then when it's time to play that game and your strength staff or your coaching staff is kind of circling that date, and guys start thinking about it all offseason and as they prepare in the summer. All those things build up, and sometimes bad things happen."

Other factors elevate the Florida-Miami series toward the top of the list of heated college football rivalries. In addition to jockeying for Top 10 and national title status, particularly in the 1980s and '90s, the schools built their powerhouses on the foundation of talent-rich Florida high school football. The recruiting wars were every bit as fierce as the battles on the field, and once the players reached the college level they found themselves battling old friends and high school rivals.

Former Miami receiver and star return man Devin Hester said many players approached it this way: "I felt like I should have gone there, and now I get a chance to play one-on-one in the game, so I'm going to destroy you. That's what makes the rivalry so great, because everybody knows each other. The guys played each other in high school and some felt like maybe they should have gone to the other school, and now they have a chance to show that they're better."

"The in-state aspect of it helps," former Miami lineman Eric Winston said. "Obviously you've got a lot of guys who know each other and a lot of pride on the line . . . a lot of Florida pride on the line. But I think it has a lot to do with a lot of good football, a lot of good players, and a lot of great games. And I think that's really what makes the rivalry great. That's why everybody remembers those games."

Pride extends well beyond the players, students, and alumni, too. Several pointed to a geographic and even cultural rivalry between South Florida and the northern expanse of the state as a contributing factor in why Gators fans love beating the Canes, and vice versa.

Miami is fast-paced South Beach, fine dining, nightclubs, art deco, and Latin-influenced culture. North of Broward and Dade counties, the remainder of the state varies from small towns, tourist destinations, beaches, city centers, Everglades swampland, and stretches of the Deep South. Gainesville is an unassuming college town of some 127,000 residents. Miami is . . . Miami.

"The one thing that's unique about Florida too is that it's almost like two different states when you begin to talk about South Florida and North Florida," said Meyer, who like all Florida and Miami coaches recruited exhaustively in both areas. "There's a lot of pride in each side of the state.

"Once you cross into Broward and Dade County, it's like a whole different state. It's South Florida. I think it's kind of cool that the rivalry is that strong. There's a strong rivalry between the two parts of the state. You can see a difference in the kids . . . a difference in the high school programs. I'm not saying one is better than the other. They're both great. But you just see a different swagger, a difference in each program when you go down into South Florida as opposed to North Florida."

"In our case," said Dickey from the Gators' perspective, "a lot of South Florida [Gators] fans who don't come to Gainesville regularly went to that game [in Miami]. There's a large turnout of Florida fans. It's like Tennessee playing in Memphis once a year or every other year or so. They get a nice turnout. So for Florida, playing in Miami brought out a great turnout of folks. I thought that helped make it a real great rivalry for us to have our fans travel, and have so many South Florida fans able to get tickets and get in the game."

Of course, that game no longer exists as a regular spot on the schedule, though the teams have agreed on a 2019 game to be played in Orlando. Florida cited SEC scheduling commitments when it dropped Miami after the 1987 season. With eight conference games and a date with perennial power (and fellow public state school) Florida State on the schedule every year, it would require a large commitment—and a dramatic change of heart—for the Gators to resume a regular home-and-home series with the Hurricanes.

Florida fans seem more willing to accept the status quo in favor of chasing SEC titles and national championship contention, while Miami followers are more adamant about wanting Florida back on the schedule. But opinions vary drastically.

"I'm frustrated by it because it doesn't make any sense," Winston said. "I understand there's conference politics and things like that, but Florida State and Florida have always figured it out. I think it's fun for the state to have that kind of state championship that we did there for a couple of years. I think it's great for recruits seeing teams play."

Mike Pouncey, Florida's former All-America lineman, said the fact the schools don't play each other every year might even add to the bad blood when they do face off. "We play Florida State every year," he said. "We're guaranteed to play them. With Miami, we play them maybe once every five years. So those guys have bragging rights for those five years. And in college football, it's all about bragging rights. Who gets the last word?"

And at least one close follower of the series doesn't find himself clamoring for more Florida-Miami confrontations at all.

"I think it's got too much vitriol in it," Dooley said of the series. "Maybe it's The Flop's fault. But it goes back even before that. You know, Steve Spurrier's last game after winning the Heisman [Trophy] was a loss to Miami, and I think that stuck with him. I think it got too nasty and too personal at times.

"It doesn't bother me that they're not playing [regularly] anymore. You know, it's funny, when I watch FSU and Miami play, I look at Gator fans in South Florida—and I have relatives down there—they root so hard for Florida State. And I'm like, 'What are you doing? How can you root for Florida State?' Well, they hate Miami that much. It's probably similar to Alabama and Auburn, without a lot of real good history.

"The hatred level is so high."

The coming chapters explore the great games, coaches, players and characters that have made the Florida-Miami rivalry what it is—venomous and heated, even when on hold.

1

"GATOR HATER" DRAWS FIRST BLOOD

NO ACCOUNT OF the Florida-Miami rivalry is complete without an ode to Walter Raymond Kichefski, the Hurricanes' original "Gator Hater." As a player, Kichefski helped Miami capture the very first game in the series on October 15, 1938, in Gainesville. He went on to coach the Hurricanes in several capacities, including a stint as head coach in 1970, and dedicated no less than fifty-six years of his life to Miami football. One constant in each of those years was his loathing of the Gators. In fact, Walt usually reduced the nickname of *that school in Gainesville* to the singular "Gator," with purposeful contempt.

"The Gator has always been a big game for us ever since the fall of 1938, when I personally played on a football team that went up [to Gainesville] to fight the Gator," Kichefski said in 1970. "Since then it's always been the big

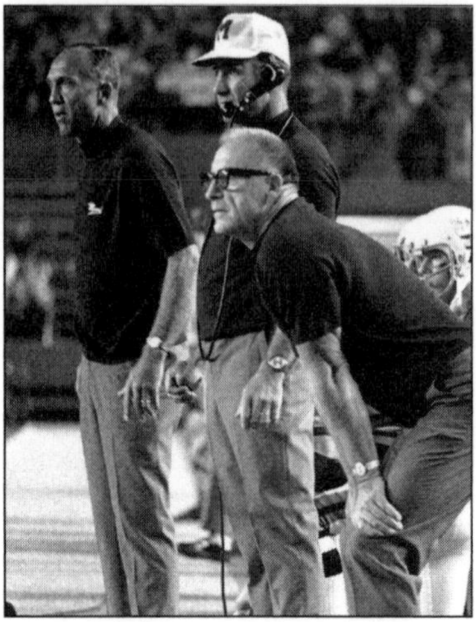

Walt Kichefski (center) coached the University of Miami for only nine games, including this 18–11 victory over Maryland at the Orange Bowl in 1970, but he had a lasting impact on the program. He famously referred to his rivals from Gainesville as "The Gator." *AP Photo*

game here at the University of Miami."[1]

"The Gator" was expecting to defeat visiting Miami in that initial meeting in 1938. After all, Florida football had a two-decade head start on its South Florida counterpart. The Gators began playing football in 1906. Between 1911 and 1930, they were almost unbeatable at home, winning 85 percent of their games. Most of those wins were on the books before the Hurricanes played their first game in 1926.

By the time the Hurricanes came to town in 1938, tiny old Fleming Field had been replaced by the University of Florida's first and only permanent football stadium, Florida Field. Miami had won each of its two previous games that season, but those were mere warm-ups against Spring Hill and Tampa. The Gators, meanwhile, got off to a rocky start with losses to Stetson and Mississippi State before righting

[1]Larry Milan, "Why Do We Hate 'The Gator'?," *SB Nation*, September 4, 2013.

their ship with a 10–6 win over Sewanee the week before the Hurricanes came to town.

"When the Hurricanes of 1938 whipped Spring Hill, nary an eyebrow was raised," penned *Miami News* columnist Jack Bell. "When they trampled Tampa, there was rejoicing among the uninitiated, but the experts admitted that it didn't take much ball club to beat the Spartans, anyway.

"When Miami smashed the Florida Gators, there was a roar of astonished delight that rattled against the Mason-Dixon Line, and caused mild flutterings of front sport pages in New York, Chicago, Detroit, and other cities of the hinterland."[2]

Perhaps the flutterings were even felt in Kichefski's hometown of Rhinelander, Wisconsin. The standout end, who would go on to play briefly in the National Football League, had no idea what to expect when his Hurricanes traveled north to Gainesville. Neither did some 3,500 Miami fans, although their hopes were high that a win over the state's established football program would have folks talking about the Hurricanes.

Interestingly enough, at least one newspaper account of the game offered some foreshadowing of events to come. "The Hurricanes breezed into Gainesville the morning of

---

[2]Jack Bell, "We Had Thrills Galore," University of Miami football yearbook, 1939.

October 14," wrote George Walsh, "behaved themselves that night, and the next evening, led by captain Eddie Dunn and a fighting spirit, they promptly muzzled the surprised Gators."[3] The fact it was deemed newsworthy that the UM players behaved themselves before the game makes the 1938 edition of the rivalry seem almost as contemporary as any of the brash and boisterous teams that came along fifty years later.

On the field, Florida's very first intrastate battle between major colleges was a well-matched affair. The game was scoreless until late in the second quarter, when Pat Reen, John Plombo, and Bud Taylor moved the Gators downfield with the help of the forward pass—not an oft-used tactic in those days. Taylor ran the ball to the Miami 18-yard line and from there connected with Plombo on a touchdown strike that, after a successful extra point kick, gave the hosts a 7–0 lead at halftime.

Whatever Miami coach Jack Harding told his troops at halftime, their early deficit would be long forgotten by the time they returned to the locker room at the end of the game. Dunn, who eased up in practice the week before the game while nursing two bad ankles, fielded a short Florida punt in the third quarter and returned it 27 yards to the Gator 28-yard line. He rambled 13 yards to put the Hurricanes

---

[3]George Walsh, "Hurricane Hits Gainesville," University of Miami football yearbook, 1939.

within a whiff of the goal line, had an apparent touchdown scamper called back due to a false start penalty, and two plays later made the infraction a moot point by practically walking in from the 2. Dunn's missed extra point kept the Gators on top, 7–6, but the score wouldn't stay that way for long.

Stout Miami defense gave the Hurricanes great field position once again, and once again Dunn ran into the end zone untouched, this time with the help of a terrific block by Andy Csaky. Armed with a 12–7 lead and all the momentum, the Hurricanes refused to let up.

Dunn completed passes to Johnny Douglas and Csaky on the Hurricanes' third and final scoring drive, which culminated with Dunn's third touchdown run—from the 1—with a few minutes remaining in the game. It was official. Miami had scored the last nineteen points of the game for a 19–7 triumph over "the Gator," as Kichefski would go on to describe the boys from Gainesville for years to come.

It was one of six losses in 11 games (4–6–1) that season for Florida. Coach Josh Cody did improve on his SEC record from his first two seasons at the helm, going 2–2–1 in the conference with a late-season win over Auburn. But the start of the rivalry with Miami left the boys from Gainesville seeking redemption.

Miami's celebration, wrote Walsh, was "for a bunch of boys that took the word *quit* out of the dictionary in a great second-half stand that netted three touchdowns—that left

15,000 fans stunned, and lifted Miami to Florida grid heights."[4]

"All this is history now," Harding expressed after a season in which his Hurricanes went on to claim the Southern Intercollegiate Athletic Association championship with an 8–2 record. "The bright feature of the whole season was the fact that we had boys we hadn't counted on rising to the heights just when they were needed. And the team spirit was marvelous—the best in my history of coaching. . . . It was swell the way the people of Miami caught onto the spirit of our team and supported them in such an admirable way."[5]

Dunn, the player who made the greatest impact in that first game between the Gators and Hurricanes, scored 15 touchdowns on the season, played in the prestigious North-South All-Star Game on New Year's Day, and went on to be named an assistant coach for Miami following the season.

Meanwhile, Kichefski was named the best defensive end in the state while also earning praise for his pass catching and blocking on the offensive side of scrimmage. That was before he earned what Miami fans consider his highest honor: the "Original Gator Hater." He would be a thread woven through the rivalry until his death in 1992.

---

[4]Ibid.

[5]Jack Harding, "The Team," University of Miami football yearbook, 1939.

The Kichefski File

Name: Walter Raymond Kichefski

Born: June 17, 1916, Rhinelander, Wisconsin

Died: January 9, 1992, Miami, Florida

Playing career: University of Miami, Pittsburgh Steelers (1940–42), Chicago Cardinals/Pittsburgh Steelers combined NFL team (1944)

Head coaching career: University of Miami (1970)

2

GATORS RULE "THE SWAMP"

THE MAN MOST responsible for the existence of "The Swamp," the University of Florida's famed home for football, was a native of Tennessee, played football for Vanderbilt—a Southeastern Conference rival of the Gators—and was athletic director and coach for another SEC rival, Kentucky. For nineteen years, however, John J. Tigert served as UF's third president, and it was under his leadership that Florida Field became home to the emerging Gator football program, and one of the best home-field advantages in the country.

The Florida Board of Control put Tigert at the helm in 1928, during a rough economic period in Florida. The "Roaring Twenties" had given way to trying times in the latter part of the decade, and one year later the Great Wall Street Crash had America in the midst of its worst economic depression. Still, Tigert proved relentless when it came to his stadium dream. Truth be told, he wasn't looking for a stadium at all. He was aiming higher. He wanted a center for celebration, school spirit, and community pride.

"The stadium has become the means of unifying the best in American college life," he said shortly after his arrival on campus. "No American university can grow in numbers or spirit, as it should, without a stadium as an adequate forum for the expression of its community of effort, spirit and activity."[1]

The Gators had played at nondescript Fleming Field since starting their program in 1906. It was really no more than an open field along West University Avenue in Gainesville in the early years, before a 1911 makeover included permanent bleachers and a rededication in former Governor Francis P. Fleming's honor. The bleachers gave it a capacity of nearly 5,000. It was adequate for most contests between 1911 and 1930, but the bigger games were often moved to larger facilities in Tampa, Jacksonville, and even Miami.

Tigert's intellect was brilliant, and his resolve legendary. Calling him a visionary was an understatement. He was Phi Beta Kappa and Vanderbilt's first Rhodes Scholar while also starring in the backfield. Before coming to Florida, he served as U.S. Commissioner of Education. He was also responsible

---

[1]David Stirt, "Tigert Understood the Significance of Sports," *Gainesville Sun*, January 26, 2005.

for devising and implementing the athletic grant-in-aid program that has helped countless student-athletes play collegiate sports while earning higher education degrees.

It turns out his timing was also impeccable, the Great Depression notwithstanding. In building support for a football stadium, it helps to have a team worthy of showcasing in the new digs. In 1928, UF came within one game of a possible national championship. Charlie Bachman, in his first year as head coach, engineered the greatest season in school history up to that point. The Gators rolled to eight consecutive victories to open the year and only one of them was a close game—a 14–7 win over North Carolina State in Jacksonville.

With SEC and national championship hopes on the line, UF lost a heartbreaking finale at Tennessee, 13–12, but Gainesville was giddy over the Gators. Now all Tigert needed was a little over $100,000—a good chunk of money in those days—to construct the stadium he wanted. There would be no public funding during the financial crisis, so the school president and ten other school supporters took out personal loans to raise the cash. Ground was broken on April 16, 1930. Less than seven months later, Florida Field—capacity 21,769—opened its gates on October 27 and hosted its first college football game two weeks later when Alabama came to town for homecoming.

"The Swamp" comes by its name naturally. It is a hole in the ground in the middle of the state, isolated from any refreshing winds from the Gulf of Mexico or the Atlantic Ocean. Its construction workers were concerned about Central Florida's low water table when building a stadium in a ravine, but underground culverts were the root of an ahead-of-its-time drainage system and any flooding problems were solved.

Heat and humidity are the norm at Florida games, and don't think teams handle it equally. While Miami is accustomed to the climate, the moist, heavy air is oppressive to most visitors. In addition to the first level of seating being located underground, those seats are a mere ten feet from

Year after year, Florida's Ben Hill Griffin Stadium ranks among the most challenging venues for road teams. From its "Gator Chomps" to the stifling heat, "The Swamp"—not to mention the Gators who play there—makes life difficult for the visitors. *AP Photo/Phelan M. Ebenhack*

the field in some spots. The stadium rises steeply and has a daunting feel for enemy schools, especially for the claustrophobic, as if 90,000 Florida fans are bearing down on their every move. It's why the stadium has been ranked among the most difficult places to play in college football.

The Gators' home record of 113 victories against 13 losses between 1990 and 2010 was the best in the nation. Head coaches Steve Spurrier and Urban Meyer lost just five games apiece at The Swamp in a combined eighteen seasons.

Each game opens with footage of alligators gathering in a Florida swamp showcased on the video board, eventually zooming in on a powerful jaw as the players take the field. The *Jaws* theme, needless to say, is a staple at Gators home games. From the loud orange walls in the corners of the complex screaming GATOR COUNTRY and THE SWAMP to the singing (and swaying) of "We Are the Boys from Old Florida" between the third and fourth quarters, the Gators' home field has an aura all its own.

"There is no better place than 'The Swamp,'" commentator Lee Corso once said. "That opening on the big screen with the alligators, it's the best ever. When the Gators run out of the tunnel, it is absolutely the moment of moments in college football."[2]

---

[2]The University of Florida official facilities website, "Ben Hill Griffin Stadium," Accessed February 12, 2016, http://floridagators.com/facilities/?id=1

It took a while for The Swamp to become the venue it is today. The original Florida Field consisted of thirty-two rows on three sides. Two decades later, in 1950, the first major renovation almost doubled the capacity to slightly more than 40,000. Lights accompanied that upgrade, and the first night game was played against The Citadel that year.

Capacity topped 60,000 in the mid-'60s thanks to the addition of permanent seats on the east side and bleachers in the south end zone. In 1982, those south end zone bleachers gave way to double-deck stands that allowed thousands more to watch games. The "Sunshine Seats" (upper deck in the north end zone) and the addition of club seats and luxury boxes since then have expanded the stadium—renamed Ben Hill Griffin Stadium in 1989 to honor a citrus magnate and generous UF financial supporter—to accommodate more than 90,000 fans on game day.

Those 90,000 truly shake the rafters of Ben Hill Griffin Stadium (the field itself is still called Florida Field, and most just say "The Swamp"). The decibel level was once recorded at 115, the equivalent of standing next to an operating sandblaster and just shy of the official threshold of pain.

"This is The Swamp," receiver Ahmad Fulwood said in 2015. "It's 90,000 and gets louder than any place in the world. It's a hard place to play at. . . . We feel like The Swamp is ours and no one is going to come and beat us on our home field. We're there to protect The Swamp."[3]

Somewhere, John J. Tigert is beaming.

Ben Hill Griffin Stadium

Tale of the Tape
Opened: October 27, 1930
Capacity: 88,548
Playing surface: Grass

[3]Robbie Andreu, "Gators Out to Protect Home Field," *Gainesville Sun*, September 2, 2015.

3

ORANGE BOWL WELCOMES UF

ONE OF THE most important and iconic sporting venues in U.S. history, the Orange Bowl was truly a place where legends were made. The fixture of Miami's Little Havana neighborhood hosted five Super Bowls, no less than eleven college football national championship celebrations, Olympic soccer contests, historic boxing matches, epic concerts, and more. A fifty-year-old Satchel Paige once pitched there.

Its longest-tenured resident was the University of Miami football team, which played within its hallowed walls from the stadium's opening in 1937 until its demolition in 2008. Originally named Burdine Stadium after Burdines department store magnate and Miami civic leader Roddy Burdine, the Orange Bowl was built thanks to a contract between UM and the city. It cost less than $350,000 to build, featured lights for night play, and seated more than 23,000—spacious compared to the Hurricanes' prior homes, Tamiami and Moore Parks.

The lights proved critical for several reasons. Although day games were still the norm, night games helped take the edge off the South Florida heat for weary combatants. They also allowed the venue to make a little history. For example, the 1965 Orange Bowl game became the first college football bowl game ever televised in prime time.

The Orange Bowl game debuted in 1935 at Miami Field and moved three years later to the venue that would later adopt its name. That 1938 contest drew 19,000 fans—approximately the combined attendance of the first three games. The game quickly became a staple of the national college bowl lineup—a position it still holds today. The stadium eventually took on the name of its most important annual event, being christened the Orange Bowl in 1959.

However, it was another trophy that had the attention of the state's college football fans in 1939. The Lou Chesna Memorial Trophy, named after a sophomore Miami fullback who had died the year before, would be awarded to the winner of the rematch between Florida and Miami at the Orange Bowl on November 18. That winning team would be declared state champion.

Miami, which had stunned Florida in Gainesville the year before in the first-ever meeting between the schools, had high hopes on its home turf. Orange Bowl capacity was stretched to the limit, with 26,000 fans on hand for Homecoming. The Hurricanes had won four of their last five games and roared into the UF contest off back-to-back wins over Texas Tech and Drake. Florida, on the other hand, had lost two straight at the hands of South Carolina and Georgia.

The Gators, however, had one distinct advantage—the memory of the previous year's loss. "It appears that the Gator has a memory like an elephant," read the Miami yearbook account of the game, "for the thought of revenge must have motivated him very strongly. Much too strongly for a gay crowd celebrating Miami's biggest Homecoming."[1]

The Hurricanes struggled to hold on to the football and were pinned deep in their own territory for much of the game thanks to well-placed "quick kicks" by the Gators. And after a scoreless first half, the visitors from Gainesville took the lead early in the third quarter and added to it in the fourth on the way to a 13–0 shutout of the Hurricanes. Quarterback Red Harrison engineered both touchdown drives, capping the first one with a 25-yard touchdown pass and using both his passing and running prowess to set up a short touchdown that put the game out of reach.

The temporary disappointment did not stop Miami fans from gobbling up tickets in the coming years. As the team, and football in general, became more popular the Orange Bowl was forced to grow, too. Some 10,000 seats were added

---

[1]1939 Miami Football Yearbook, "Sad Homecoming."

in the end zones to enclose the complex in 1944. Just three years later, another 25,000 seats arrived to stretch capacity past 60,000.

The 1950s saw further expansion to more than 75,000, where the stadium would teeter (with subtle variation) for the rest of its existence. The National Football League's Miami Dolphins debuted at the Orange Bowl in 1966 and played there until moving to their own facility two decades later. The Orange Bowl hosted back-to-back Super Bowl games in 1968 and '69 and three more in the 1970s, including the Pittsburgh Steelers' 21–17 win over the Dallas Cowboys in Super Bowl X that drew more than 80,000 patrons.

Even more collegiate national champions than Super Bowl winners were crowned under the lights of the Orange Bowl. As fate would have it, the Hurricanes clinched three of their five national titles (or co-titles) between 1983 and 2001 on their home turf. They beat Nebraska in the Orange Bowl for championships in '83 and '91 and did the same to Oklahoma in '87.

Both the Hurricanes and Dolphins gave the Orange Bowl a legitimate case as providing one of the greatest home-field advantages in sports during two long stretches. UM set an NCAA record by winning 58 consecutive home games between 1985 and '94, while the Dolphins had given the stadium its first glorious run with 31 straight home wins between 1971 and '74.

For seven decades until its demolition in 2008, the Miami Hurricanes called the Orange Bowl home. The iconic venue was originally called Burdine Stadium until it was renamed for the college football bowl game that was annually played there. *AP Photo/Lynne Sladky*

Miami games became renowned for the team's entrance onto the field through a smoke-filled tunnel and a swagger meant to leave visitors intimidated before the game even reached the coin toss. They began calling themselves by a single letter—"The U"—and they were loud enough, and dominant enough, to make it stick.

"We're all from that area we basically grew up in Miami [as] Hurricane fans," said Devin Hester, one of the leaders during the Canes' dominant era. "You watch them on TV and then you get a chance to play a game in the Orange Bowl . . . it's like a dream come true for an athlete who grew up down south."

As time passed, state-of-the-art stadiums around the country far surpassed the Orange Bowl in amenities, player facilities, comfort, sight lines, technology, and the like. As revered as the stadium's history is and will always be, large numbers of fans wanted ambiance—seat backs, clean restrooms, and better food options, among other perks, for their hard-earned dollar.

The longtime Orange Bowl diehards hated to see their stadium go, but the Dolphins had moved to their own brand new stadium after the 1986 season, and twenty-one years later the Hurricanes followed suit. Their final game in the Orange Bowl was one they would rather forget—a 48–0 loss to Virginia in front of several former Hurricane stars in November 2007—but their stay was a hugely successful one.

"You know, you've got progress everywhere," said former Hurricanes coach Jimmy Johnson, "and I think it was good for the University of Miami to move up to Dolphin Stadium. I think the facilities will be so much nicer. Without question, there's always going to be nostalgia for the Orange Bowl, and great memories. But I don't think we'll ever lose that."[2]

Marlins Park, the home of baseball's Miami Marlins, now stands where the Orange Bowl once did. As a tribute to the

---

[2]Accord Productions, "The Orange Bowl Stadium Movie," December 18, 2008, accessed January 18, 2016, https://www.youtube.com/watch?v=oGckl4JWR98

old stadium, the 10-foot-tall orange letters that used to spell "Miami Orange Bowl" were arranged by a local artist to spell different words on the east plaza of the baseball park.

The Orange Bowl

Tale of the Tape

Opened: December 10, 1937

Demolished: May 14, 2008

Capacity: 72,319

Playing surface: Grass

4

UPSETS, WAR, AND THE 1940s

"YOU CAN THROW the records out the window when these teams play." The notion that anything can happen, regardless of the teams' records, is a common adage when it comes to sports rivalries. It's built on a theory that the underdog is so motivated to "rise up" against a bitter rival that the favorite's superior talent, or superior scheme, or superior coaching will not necessarily win out.

It did not take long for the Florida-Miami rivalry to qualify as Exhibit A. Following UM's upset win in the series' 1938 opener, Florida had rebounded to win two straight, including a 46–6 rout in Miami in 1940. That one was no contest, as the score indicated, and had followers of the Gators shrugging off the notion that anyone could challenge them for state bragging rights.

But along came 1941, and even the most ardent UF fan had to be nervous about a November 15 trip to Miami. Under Coach Jack Harding, the Hurricanes had not only shaken off that previous year's drubbing at the hands of Florida, they had raced to the best start in school history. Harding's boys easily handled four overmatched opponents to open the year, and then made a grand statement with a 6–0 win over Texas Tech on Halloween Day. A 34–0 thumping of West Virginia Wesleyan gave them a spotless 6–0 record with the Gators coming to town.

Florida, on the other hand, was reeling. Second-year head coach Tom Lieb had dropped the final two games of 1940 and was off to a 2–5 start in '41, including four straight losses entering the Miami game. In six of those seven losses dating back to the previous season, his Gators had scored seven points or less. They had been shut out entirely in three of them.

Throw out the records? Well, yes, thanks mainly to Tommy "Red" Harrison and Forest Ferguson. Harrison was well on his way to a Florida career record for total offensive yards (2,133) that would stand for twenty-four years until Steve Spurrier broke it. Ferguson set receiving records that stood until the 1960s, and is considered one of the greatest athletes to ever compete for UF. He was a 205-pounder who could outrun defensive backs or pummel opposing ballcarriers with equal proficiency, and also starred in boxing and track and field.

Harrison connected with Ferguson on touchdown passes of 44 and 74 yards to lead the Gators to a convincing 14–0 win at the Orange Bowl, called Burdine Stadium at the time, in front of 31,731 fans. "No more outstanding player has appeared here this year than the indomitable Ferguson," the Associated Press wrote in its game recap. "Not only did he make those two touchdowns, but he had the biggest hand in stifling Miami's offensive."[1] The *Miami Herald* listed the score: "Forrest Ferguson 14; University of Miami 0."

The heroes in that game, Ferguson and Harrison, were among several players from both schools who became heroes in a far more important venue—the battlefield in World War II. Both earned distinction as U.S. Army officers. Ferguson was honored with the Distinguished Service Cross for his heroism on the beaches of Normandy on "D-Day" in 1944. Tragically, he also suffered a serious head wound from which he never recovered. "Fergie" died ten years later. The Fergie Ferguson Award is now given to the UF senior football player who displays outstanding leadership, character, and courage.

The Hurricanes ended their three-game slump in the series with a 12–0 home shutout of the Gators in 1942. It was another great year for Harding and Miami, particularly on defense. The Hurricanes entered the game

---

[1]Associated Press, "Miami's Perfect Record Is Smeared by Gators," *St. Petersburg Times,* November 16, 1941.

yielding an average of just 93 yards from scrimmage—tops in the nation.

The Gators exceeded that with 176 yards and had every chance to win the game. However, two fumbles and a key penalty deep in Miami territory stalled three drives without UF getting on the scoreboard. For the Canes, it was the running of Bob McDougal and Al Kasulin that made the difference. McDougal, a bruiser, accounted for 56 of his team's 79 yards on a second-quarter touchdown march that ended with Kasulin charging into the end zone from the 2. McDougal added a short scoring burst of his own in the fourth quarter to seal the victory before a modest Miami crowd of about 15,000.

The nation had other interests in the mid-1940s, of course. The war depleted college football teams throughout the land, and Florida and Miami were no exceptions. Neither school fielded a team in 1943. When they resumed in 1944, they did so with many of their best athletes wearing different uniforms: those of U.S. military branches. That included the head coach in UM's case, as Eddie Dunn—the former great who scored all three Hurricane touchdowns in the very first meeting between these schools—filled in for Harding in '44.

The dearth of talent was most evident on the Miami side during that '44 clash with the Gators. The Hurricanes had not scored a point in any of their first three games, and the November 3 homecoming date against Florida did nothing to change that. UM fumbles set up both UF touchdowns—runs by Bobby Forbes and Ken McLean—in a 13–0 Gator victory at the Orange Bowl.

Harding returned from the war to the Miami sideline the following year, and not a moment too soon for Hurricanes fans. The result was the greatest one-year turnaround in program history, as Miami jumped from 1–7–1 in 1944 to 9–1–1 and Orange Bowl champs in '45. Included among those nine wins was a spectacular 7–6 decision against Lieb's final Florida squad on October 19.

Both touchdowns were impressive, and the drama of the extra point attempts was unrivaled. A capacity Orange Bowl crowd of 27,000 was riveted by the mayhem, and most went home in wild celebration after one of the craziest games anyone had ever witnessed.

Miami marched 63 yards for a touchdown on the first possession, with fullback Harry Ghaul scampering in from the 12-yard-line. The extra point kick was blocked by the Gators, but Ghaul alertly picked up the ball and lateraled it to halfback Ernie Mazejka, who crossed the goal line for the point and a 7–0 Hurricanes lead.

Five Miami fumbles—three recovered by the Gators—kept Florida in the hunt, and in the third quarter the visitors broke through in a big way. Angus Williams fielded a Ghaul punt and sprinted 48 yards to the end zone, putting UF within one point of tying the game. Once again, that extra point try became an adventure.

Just as Florida had done earlier, Miami blocked the kick. This time, however, an offsides penalty against UM gave Florida another chance. The Gators opted to run for the point rather than trying another kick, and gave the ball to Williams. Swiftly and surely, Bill Levitt came flying in for the Hurricanes, stopping Williams short of the line and preserving the 7–6 outcome.

That classic began a home-and-home schedule between the schools that brought the rivalry back to Gainesville in 1946 for the first time since the initial meeting eight years earlier. It was homecoming for UF and many in the crowd of 21,000 took to chanting "Gator bait!" toward the visitors, but Miami overcame a 13–7 halftime deficit to win 20–13. UF's lead was built on a sensational 97-yard punt return for a touchdown by freshman Hal Griffin, who tightroped the sideline without stepping out of bounds.

However, the second half was all Miami. Bill Krasnai ran for a third-quarter touchdown and Ghaul's extra point kick put the Hurricanes on top 14–13. Krasnai added another score as time expired in the contest. Harding's Hurricanes, the defending Orange Bowl champs, were on their way to another terrific year, while Raymond Wolf was in his first season at the Florida helm. It would take him until the following autumn to win his first game, when his 4–5–1 mark included a 7–6 triumph in Miami to spoil the Hurricanes' homecoming weekend.

That was the farewell season for Harding at the Miami helm, as Andy Gustafson took over the following year. Harding had won a combined 17 games in his first two years back from the war, but slipped to 2–7–1 during that 1947 season.

Finally, in 1948, the Gators managed to beat Miami for the first time in Gainesville. It was another homecoming contest and took place in front of the largest crowd in school history—more than 27,000, many of whom did not even have a place to sit. Most were on their feet in the early going anyway, as the Gators sprinted to a quick lead and never trailed. Charlie Hunsinger scored two UF touchdowns, while John Cox and Fal Johnson added one apiece.

It was a noteworthy game not only because it was Florida's first-ever home win over Miami, but also because it gave an early indication as to what fans could expect when UF and UM took the field. Hard feelings had been building up in these annual homecoming weekend state championship tilts. Florida State's program was just one year old and would not face Florida or Miami until the 1950s, so media outlets loudly declared the victor of the UF-UM game the state title winner. The Hurricanes were hit with three personal foul penalties and the Gators one in the late minutes of the clash,

---

[2]Dan Hall, "Florida Gators Whip Hurricanes, 27 to 13," *St. Petersburg Times*, November 21, 1948.

and a Miami player was ejected for unsportsmanlike conduct. Foreshadowing?

"The game was complete with the state's big political guns, bands, drum majorettes, display card formations, Miami Hurricane warning flags and a few fights, on and off the field," wrote Dan Hall in the *St. Petersburg Times*.[2]

Wolf was unable to close his Florida coaching career, or the 1940s, with three wins in a row against Miami. His Gators ran into a revitalized Hurricanes team—and a regular-season record crowd of 55,981 at the Orange Bowl—and fell by a 28–13 score. Halfback Mike Vacchio carried 20 times for 140 yards to lead the Hurricanes, who darted to an early 14–0 lead and then pulled away with two more touchdowns in the fourth quarter.

Miami was a sophomore-dominated team that went on to a 6–3 record, leaving Gustafson and those 55,000-plus fans thrilled about their prospects as the 1950s loomed. Florida was optimistic, too, after it was announced that Bob Woodruff would be taking the coaching reins in 1950. The second half of the twentieth century had arrived, and so too had a pair of college football programs that were growing up quickly, as their contempt for each other grew as well.

Florida-Miami in the 1940s

Date	Location	Winner	Score
November 16, 1940	Miami, FL	Florida	46–6
November 15, 1941	Miami, FL	Florida	14–0
November 14, 1942	Miami, FL	Miami	12–0
November 3, 1944	Miami, FL	Florida	13–0
October 19, 1945	Miami, FL	Miami	7–6
October 19, 1946	Gainesville, FL	Miami	20–13
November 22, 1947	Miami, FL	Florida	7–6
November 20, 1948	Gainesville, FL	Florida	27–13
November 18, 1949	Miami, FL	Miami	28–13

5

HARDING LEAVES LASTING IMPACT

THE UNIVERSITY OF Miami's first prominent football coach was, by one measure and one measure alone, a failure in what he set out to do at the South Florida school. "We haven't been able to change Miami's green and white to blue and gold yet," Jack Harding, a University of Pittsburgh graduate, joked with a Pittsburgh reporter in 1948, referring to his alma mater's school colors. "But give us time."[1]

That time never arrived, despite Harding's long tenure with the green-clad Hurricanes. He coached them to a 54–32–3 record over nine seasons beginning in 1937, missing the 1943 and 1944 campaigns while serving with distinction in World War II. He then worked as athletic director for fifteen

---

[1]Carl Hughes, "Yes, Florida Has Grid Players But Northern Crop Looks Good," *Pittsburgh Post-Gazette*, July 22, 1948.

years until his death in 1963. During that time, he lifted Miami on a national scale in virtually every varsity sport.

As a football coach, Harding demanded excellence but did so in a positive, nurturing manner. After all, the program was in just its second year of existence when he brought a 49–37–9 record from Scranton University in his native Pennsylvania. There was plenty of nurturing to be done.

Harding did so using a wise mix of recruits from his home state and Florida. One of his last Miami teams had twenty former Pennsylvania high school standouts on the roster. Back then, Florida had not yet earned its elite status on the recruiting trail compared with some of the northern states, so Harding lured some of the better talent south. The allure of year-round football, sunshine, and beaches helped his cause.

"No section has a monopoly on quality," he said. "But Pennsylvania has a monopoly on quantity. We have six schools in Florida competing for talent. On the other hand, there isn't the same proportion of boys playing high school football down there that there is around Pittsburgh, for instance. At least there aren't enough to go around."[2]

That began to change somewhat during Harding's time at the UM helm, and he took advantage by building strong teams with homegrown talent, too. Before he dedicated two years to the U.S. Navy as an officer, he led the Hurricanes to a pair of 8–2 seasons and one 7–2 slate. His 1938 team is

---

[2]Ibid.

considered one of the best in school history. In his first year back from the war in 1945, he guided the Hurricanes to a 9–1–1 record that included wins over Michigan State, North Carolina State, Auburn, Florida, Clemson, and a thrilling 13–6 Orange Bowl victory over Holy Cross that still ranks among that bowl game's all-time classic finishes. The following season, the Canes went 8–2.

Miami should have expected such success when they landed the man many called "Spike." A three-sport star at Pittsburgh, he played for legendary coach Glenn "Pop" Warner and was a promising minor league baseball player in the St. Louis Cardinals system. Coaching, however, had his heart, so he followed that path over his baseball aspirations. Once it led him to Coral Gables, Harding had found a permanent home.

In addition to upgrading the Hurricanes on the football field and across the spectrum of athletics during his decades-long dedication to the school, one of Harding's biggest successes came in choosing his head coaching successor. He turned to an old buddy. Andy Gustafson was his close friend and backfield mate at Pittsburgh during the 1920s, and had been coaching the backfield at Army when Harding contacted him following the 1947 season. Gustafson accepted the post, and the Hurricanes would not find themselves in the market for their next head coach for another sixteen seasons.

"We never thought we had a chance to get Andy," Harding said. "After I decided to devote all my time to being athletic director, the football job was thrown wide open. There were a lot of applicants, but Andy wasn't one of them. . . . We considered ourselves pretty lucky when he agreed to come to Miami."[3]

Reunited, Harding and Gustafson worked once again as a formidable pair. While Gustafson kept the football program advancing and—a big key to success in the job—held his own in the annual rivalry with the Florida Gators, Harding pushed the entire athletic department forward on other courts and playing fields. Miami's athletic department had reached the big time.

Harding's health took a turn for the worse in 1962. He underwent surgery in August, and died at age sixty-five on February 24, 1963. Cancer was the culprit. Three weeks before his death, more than 1,000 friends, family members, fellow athletic directors, and former players attended a Miami event in Harding's honor, thanking him for his contributions not only to their lives, but to college football. "We, your friends, thank you for your wonderful gift to sports," said Wally Butts, University of Georgia athletic director.[4]

"I never heard anyone say a bad word about Spike," Gustafson said. "And I'm sure that he never even thought about saying an unkind word about anyone else."[5]

---

[3]Ibid.

[4]Associated Press, "Jack Harding Is Honored," *St. Petersburg Evening Independent*, February 4, 1963.

[5]Associated Press, "Harding Dies," *Lakeland Ledger*, February 25, 1963.

Harding, who once served as state chairman for the National Football Foundation and Hall of Fame, has been inducted posthumously into several halls of fame, including the College Sports Hall of Fame (1980), University of Miami Sports Hall of Fame (1967), and Florida Sports Hall of Fame (1967). In 2009, he was inducted into the Greater Miami Chamber of Commerce Hall of Champions.

Harding is also remembered and recognized every year by the Hurricanes football program when team members —still wearing Miami green rather than Pittsburgh blue and gold—vote for their Most Valuable Player. The winner receives the Jack Harding Award, presented every year since 1964. It's considered the highest honor given by the program.

The Harding File

Name: Jack Harding
Born: January 4, 1898, Avoca, Pennsylvania
Died: February 24, 1963, Miami, Florida
Playing career: University of Pittsburgh (1924–25)
Head coaching career: St. Thomas (Pa.) (1926–36), University of Miami (1937–42 and 1945–47)
Athletic director: University of Miami (1948–63)

Note: Harding also coached college basketball at St. Thomas (Pa.) and baseball at Miami.

6

THE 1950s: WOODRUFF VS. GUSTAFSON FOR A CANOE

FLORIDA'S STATE COLLEGE football championship became a little more convoluted in the 1950s, with Florida State arriving as a third big school in the mix. That was on paper, however, rather than on the grass in Miami and Gainesville, where everyone knew the winner of the annual Florida-Miami game reigned supreme (as always) in the Sunshine State. "Florida will always be our greatest rival," proclaimed Hurricanes coach Andy Gustafson in 1955.[1]

If the 1950s are remembered as an upbeat, anything-is-possible time in United States history, the era is recalled even more fondly by those who have followed Florida and Miami football for a long time. Both schools were led by a single

[1]Associated Press, "60,000 Expected for Miami Game," *Daytona Beach Morning Journal*, November 24, 1955.

head coach during the decade—Bob Woodruff overseeing the Gators and Gustafson directing the Hurricanes. And for the first time in the history of the rivalry, you could pretty much count on both teams entering their annual game with high hopes, loads of talent, and a strong desire to knock out their in-state rival. Each school was ranked in the Associated Press Top 20 eight times during the 1950s.

"You can't make a favorite in these traditional games," Gustafson said in 1955, the year the Seminole War Canoe was donated by the City of Hollywood, Florida, to serve as the trophy awarded to the winner of the annual game. "Both teams go all out in this one, and anything can happen."[2]

The UF-UM game was played in late November throughout the 1950s, with the exception of a December 1 tussle in Gainesville in 1956. The 1950s also marked the first time when winning streaks of significance popped up in the series. Miami began a string of four wins in a row over Florida in 1953. The Gators then answered with a four-game win streak between 1957 and '60.

The teams traded wins to start the decade before the Hurricanes rattled off their four straight victories. Miami dominated the Gators before a record crowd of 40,000 at Florida Field in 1950, though the final score was a deceptive 20–14. The Canes, despite injuries to a couple of their top

---

[2]Associated Press, "Gator, Miami Classic Toss-Up—Gustafson," *Sarasota Herald-Tribune*, November 22, 1955.

players, amassed a 25–9 edge in first downs and a 240–97 advantage in rushing yards. The Gators failed to cross midfield with the football until the second half against a Miami team that ended up 9–1–1 and in the Orange Bowl.

The 1951 game was also played before a record crowd—61,602 on a chilly night in Miami. The most important spectators were representatives of the Gator Bowl in Jacksonville. They said after watching a one-sided, 21–6 Miami triumph that they would be honored to have the Canes playing in their bowl game, and they got just that. UM would go on to blank Clemson, 14–0, in that contest.

Florida had no solution for 142-pound Miami sparkplug Jack Hackett. The quarterback completed 16 of 26 passes for 224 yards, running for one touchdown and setting up the other two with his accurate throws. The Hurricanes built a 21–0 lead before easing up in the fourth quarter.

The schools were working on a new, four-year contract to continue the annual series at that time, and during the summer of 1952 tensions flared off the field. Specifically, Miami became upset that Florida went public with details of the negotiations. The Hurricanes accused Woodruff of violating their trust when the head coach pointed out in the press the discrepancy between the scholarship money UM offered its athletes compared to the lower state school costs UF covered for its players.

"It was agreed we would discuss our negotiations with our respective athletic committees," said Woodruff, who argued that Miami gave its players forty dollars per month while Florida and other SEC schools were capped at fifteen dollars per month. There was some sentiment that SEC schools, including Florida, would no longer schedule the Hurricanes unless Miami, which was not affiliated with a conference, agreed to the lower amount to level the playing field in recruiting. Continued Woodruff: "Our athletic authorities felt Florida's position had to be made known to the general public who had purchased $30,000 worth of tickets and had asked so many times why the contract hadn't been signed."[3]

Gustafson and Miami athletic director Jack Harding issued a statement that said: "When we met in Birmingham [Alabama], Aug. 18, Coach Woodruff agreed that no statements would be issued to the press until the matter was settled by both athletic committees. . . . Woodruff violated this trust and apparently tried to put Miami in an unfair position with his full statement to the press last night."[4]

The contract was signed and the series extended, and on November 22, 1952, Woodruff and the Gators appeared to take out their hard feelings over the off-field matter and their three straight losses to the Hurricanes when they ran roughshod over Miami, 43–6, at Florida Field.

---

[3]Associated Press, "Miami Officials Claim Woodruff Violated Trust," *Sarasota Herald-Tribune*, September 4, 1952.
[4]Ibid.

Halfback Buford Long scored two touchdowns and backfield mates Rick Casares, Papa Hall, and Doug Dickey added one apiece as Florida secured a berth in the Gator Bowl—the first postseason bowl game appearance in school history. Miami managed just 17 yards rushing and averted a shutout only thanks to a meaningless late touchdown. Florida, 8–3, went on to win the Gator Bowl in Woodruff's best season. The *Sarasota Herald* topped the game statistics with the headline, "Miami Needs Pay Boost."[5]

Gustafson said that Florida team had everything. As he turned his Hurricanes around, however, after a 4–7 season in 1952, he learned it would be a long while before he had to swallow another loss to the Gators. His 1953 team went 4–5 but managed a thrilling 14–10 upset of Florida, a two-touchdown favorite, with scoring drives of 61 and 57 yards in the second half at the Orange Bowl.

Whitey Rouviere ran three yards for a UM touchdown early in the second half to give the hosts, utterly dominated in the first half, a 7–3 edge. After UF regained the lead, Miami freshman fullback Ed Oliver jumped in from the 3-yard line for the winning touchdown with four minutes remaining. It was the beginning of great things for the young Hurricanes, including a four-game win streak against their greatest rivals.

---

[5]Associated Press, "Florida Whips Miami, 43-6; Host for Gator Bowl," *Sarasota Herald-Tribune*, November 23, 1952.

The 1954 Hurricanes staged a dramatic turnaround as their young talent gained seasoning. They went 8–1, were ranked as high as sixth in the AP poll and took care of the Gators, as expected, in their clash at Florida Field. They scored touchdowns in the second and third quarters and would have enjoyed an easier victory were it not for several fumbles, including ones that stopped each of their first two possessions. There were only seven Miami seniors on that team.

So when the Seminole War Canoe came around in 1955, it was logical to expect the powerful Hurricanes to paddle away in it. They did, but it wasn't easy. Even before the game, Gustafson noted that preparing for a team that knows your players so well often calls for a few updates. "You almost have to put in new plays in this situation, and we have," he explained. "They probably know every move we make. We've scouted them pretty good, too."[6]

The Gators' defensive adjustments before the '55 classic in the Orange Bowl gave a powerful Miami team fits. The Hurricanes managed just one sustained drive. Quarterback Mario Bonofiglio, who was all but benched after a miserable performance against Notre Dame earlier in the season, dissected Florida on that first-half march and scored the touchdown on a nifty keeper. Other than that, though, Gustafson's option offense was stymied like it hadn't been all year.

---

[6]Associated Press, "60,000 Expected for Miami Game," *Daytona Beach Morning Journal*, November 24, 1955.

Florida moved the football better against Miami's punishing defense than anyone all season, including the Fighting Irish. Fullback Joe Brodsky, whose injuries had relegated him to third-team duty in advance of the game, was a 218-pound buzzsaw against the Hurricanes. He powered into the end zone to make the score 7–6, but the extra-point kick was a low line drive that hit a Miami player, leaving UF a single point short. The Gators played like world-beaters on this day—well enough to prevail against most anyone but these Hurricanes.

"The score was 7–6 and this is eloquent testimony to a crystal clear fact—Miami has a great football team," wrote Bill Beck of the *St. Petersburg Times*. "This was a day on which a resounding upset might have occurred. Yet so big, strong and skilled were the Miamians that no upset happened."[7]

Miami's fourth consecutive win in the series, in 1956, was a little easier on Gustafson's heart. His team took a 14–0 lead and clinched a 20–7 decision in Gainesville when speedster Don Bosseler raced 73 yards for the final score. It was after that game that Florida's Woodruff, on his way to a 6–3–1 season, said it was time to go "Gator hunting," as in recruiting. And UF needed a canoe to do it in.

That came the following season, when the Gators finally ended Miami's four-game win streak in the series and began

[7]Bill Beck, "It's Miami Over Florida by a Foot, 7–6," *St. Petersburg Times*, November 27, 1955.

one of their own. In Miami in 1957, Wayne Williamson connected with Billy Newbern on a 39-yard pass to the Hurricanes 1-yard line and Florida star Jim Rountree pounded into the end zone from there to give the Gators all the points they would need to win at the Orange Bowl. Miami never crossed midfield in the game. Rountree's kicking also sparked UF, which scored again in the fourth quarter en route to a 14–0 shutout win.

The teams signed up for back-to-back games in Jacksonville in 1958 and '59, and most expected an easy Florida victory in the former year. Miami, which had been ranked early in the season, had faltered badly all year while the Gators were on their way to a third straight six-win campaign.

Form held for most of the game. Florida took a 12–0 lead and appeared to be cruising toward a Gator Bowl berth. A second-half Miami rally fell short, with Florida conceding a safety late in the game, but the inspired play of the Hurricanes was a refreshing sign for a strong UM contingent who made the drive up the state's Atlantic coast. Woodruff could hardly sign the Gator Bowl contract quickly enough after the close call. It was his second Gator Bowl berth as Florida coach.

The '59 rematch in Jacksonville had the Hurricanes needing a win to secure an Orange Bowl berth, but Florida's convincing 23–14 victory made it three in a row for the Gators. It was an offensive showcase for the boys from Gainesville, the highlight coming when Don Deal broke away and sprinted 70-plus yards for the clinching touchdown in the second half.

It should have been sweet retribution for Woodruff, who was riding a three-game winning streak in the series. Many Florida fans, however, wondered why the Gators hadn't been playing like that from the outset. They were itching for a change that was about to come.

Woodruff's Gators coaching career spanned the 1950s in their entirety. No more. No less. His 53 victories made him the winningest coach in Florida history. He went 4–6 against Miami and beat Florida State in the first two meetings between those schools in '58 and '59. Woodruff had earned the Gainesville faithful a coveted canoe for three straight years as state champions.

Florida-Miami in the 1950s

Date	Location	Winner	Score
November 18, 1950	Gainesville, FL	Miami	20–14
November 17, 1951	Miami, FL	Miami	21–6
November 22, 1952	Gainesville, FL	Florida	43–6
November 28, 1953	Miami, FL	Miami	14–10
November 27, 1954	Gainesville, FL	Miami	14–0
November 26, 1955	Miami, FL	Miami	7–6
December 1, 1956	Gainesville, FL	Miami	20–7
November 30, 1957	Miami, FL	Florida	14–0
November 29, 1958	Jacksonville, FL	Florida	12–9
November 28, 1959	Jacksonville, FL	Florida	23–14

7

WOODRUFF PUSHES QUIET PROGRESS

GEORGE ROBERT WOODRUFF went by "Bob," which was entirely fitting given the fact he was a man of few words. Florida's coach throughout the 1950s once called himself "the oratorical equivalent of a blocked punt."[1] There would be long periods of silence between statements. Woodruff even mastered the art of bumming cigarettes with just a nod. There was debate over whether his silence was haughty or tepid, but all could agree it matched his conservative, defensive-minded approach to football.

"Bob always had an idea he was different than anyone else in the room," offered Doug Dickey, who played under Woodruff at Florida and coached under him after Woodruff

---

[1]Mike Bianchi, "Bianchi: Spring a Time for Gators to Say Hello to Jim McElwain, Goodbye to Ray Graves," *Orlando Sentinel*, April 11, 2015.

became athletic director at his alma mater, Tennessee.[2] Added former tackle Charlie LaPradd, "You never knew if Coach Woodruff was thirty minutes ahead of you or thirty minutes behind."[3]

One thing is certain: Florida spoke loudly when it hired Woodruff to lead its football program and athletic department in 1950. They signed the thirty-four-year-old Baylor head coach to a seven-year deal worth $17,000 per year—$7,000 more than his predecessor, Raymond Wolf, had been earning. Woodruff, who had learned from some of the game's great coaches during stints as an assistant at Tennessee (Robert Neyland), Army (Earl Blaik), and Georgia Tech (Bobby Dodd), led Baylor to a 19–10–2 record over three seasons and a Dixie Bowl victory in 1948.

One of Woodruff's first orders of business in Gainesville was getting his team's grades up. When he learned that forty-seven players were carrying less than a C average, he had his staff institute every-other-week classroom progress checks. "We are working as hard on studies as we are on football practice," he said.[4]

On the field, there is no denying the forward progress the Gators made under Woodruff. Before his arrival, they

---

[2]Buddy Martin, *The Boys from Old Florida: Inside Gator Nation* (New York: Sports Publishing, 2013), 29.

[3]Ibid, 30.

[4]Dan Hall, "Everybody Likes Bob Woodruff," *St. Petersburg Times*, April 5, 1950.

had never appeared in the Associated Press rankings or competed in a bowl game. During his ten years, they cracked the Top 20 at some point during all but 1951 and earned two Gator Bowl berths, winning in 1952. His 53–42–6 record launched him atop the school's career victory list.

He rarely said much, but Bob Woodruff spoke volumes in the win column. His 53 victories in the 1950s vaulted him to the top of Florida's career wins list, and his Gators also began making regular appearances in the AP rankings. *1951 Florida Seminole via Wikimedia Commons*

The fact Woodruff was not an eloquent communicator was partially offset by the brilliance of his assistant coaches, and he certainly tutored some good ones. By that measure, he was an overwhelming success. Many went on to become head coaches themselves, including Frank Broyles (Arkansas), Dale Hall (Army), Hank Foldberg (Texas A&M), Tonto Coleman (Abilene Christian and SEC commissioner), John Rauch (Oakland Raiders and Buffalo Bills), and Charlie Tate (Miami).

"Coach Woodruff did an outstanding job of picking assistant coaches, and they stayed there with him the whole time," Dickey said. "They came from outstanding football programs, and it gave Florida a big boost. They kept us turning the corner and getting better, even though we weren't quite ready to play with the big boys."[5]

After two 5–5 seasons to begin his Florida tenure, in which he implemented his defensive-minded—some might say conservative—system, the Gators took off in 1952. Their eight wins included victories over Georgia, Auburn, and strong teams from Kentucky and Tulsa, the latter in the Gator Bowl. It was not until '56, however, that Woodruff posted his next winning record. It was the first of three consecutive six-win seasons, an improvement over the previous three years but not what Gators fans expected.

Students, alumni, and boosters began putting pressure on Florida to replace Woodruff midway through his tenure, but the university honored and eventually extended his contract. For his part, Woodruff took the pressure with grace. Perhaps his being a man of few words served him well in that regard. He said in 1955 that it was unfair for his players and assistant coaches to read in the newspapers that "they must win a certain game to hold my job for me."[6]

The Gators went 18–9–3 between '56 and '58, culminating that stretch with their second-ever bowl appearance. They dropped a 7–3 decision to Mississippi in the Gator

---

[5] *The Boys from Old Florida: Inside Gator Nation*, 32

[6] Associated Press, "Many Support Florida Coach Bob Woodruff," *Sarasota Herald-Tribune*, November 10, 1955.

Bowl that year, and coming back with a 5–4–1 mark in 1959 was not acceptable to anyone involved with the program, including Woodruff. Pressure increased for his resignation, and after the season he met with university president Dr. J. Wayne Reitz and obliged.

His resignation made way for Ray Graves, a defensive line coach at Georgia Tech, to be hired by the Gators. There were reports that Woodruff might return to his home state and the Yellow Jackets as line coach, and Dodd made it clear his one-time understudy would get close consideration should he be interested. Ultimately, Woodruff decided to return to his alma mater, Tennessee, as an assistant and eventually was promoted to athletic director.

Woodruff held that post for twenty-two years, leading the Volunteers to national success across multiple playing fields and bringing state-of-the-art facilities to Knoxville. They won national titles in track, swimming, and cross–country under his watch and played in 15 football bowl games. Woodruff also worked for the U.S. Olympic Committee for the 1972 Summer Games in Munich. When he resigned his Tennessee post in 1985, he was replaced by his former Florida Gators star, Dickey.

Woodruff, a member of the UF Athletic Hall of Fame, died in Knoxville in 2001. He was eighty-five. Two years later, his former assistant, Broyles, became the first winner of the Bob Woodruff Award, honoring outstanding work by an athletic director.

The Woodruff File

Name: George Robert Woodruff
Born: March 14, 1916, Athens, Georgia
Died: November 1, 2001, Knoxville, Tennessee
Playing career: University of Tennessee (1936–38)
Head coaching career: Baylor University (1947–49), University of Florida (1950–59)
Athletic director: University of Florida (1950–59), University of Tennessee (1963–85)

8

THE 1960s: MIAMI REELS IN A GATOR

THE 1960s TREATED Florida a little better than Miami on the football field, but that did not always show in the battle for the Seminole War Canoe. The schools each won five times in the rivalry, which seemed to be heating up by the year. An interesting twist came along in December 1963, when Miami did the unthinkable—hiring a former Gator, Charlie Tate, as head coach.

Tate had coached high school football in Miami and was the freshman coach at UF before assisting the great Bobby Dodd at Georgia Tech between 1957 and '63. When the former Gator fullback was tabbed to replace Andy Gustafson at the Miami helm, he knew the road to success would lead through his beloved alma mater, but made quick work of becoming a Hurricane.

"I worked there once before in a high school capacity and I have a lot of friends down there," Tate said of Miami. "I'm very glad to have the chance to go back and I hope I can do a good job for Miami."[1]

It was a new Florida hire, Ray Graves, who put his stamp on the UF-UM series in 1960. Graves's first Florida team was a power, and its 18–0 whitewashing at Miami on November 26 was not even as close as the final score. Bobby Dodd Jr. and Larry Libertore ran for first-half touchdowns and Don Goodman added one after the break as the Gators dominated from start to finish.

"You have to rate them with the best we've played," said Gustafson, whose 6–4 Hurricanes had also faced Pittsburgh, Auburn, Syracuse, and Notre Dame. Quipped Graves, "I think Florida ought to keep Ray Graves."[2]

Gustafson and the Hurricanes snapped a four-game losing streak against the Gators with a 15–6 win in Gainesville in 1961 and followed it up with a 17–15 decision against UF in '62. Miami had a Liberty Bowl berth already in hand when they took the '61 contest. Hurricanes quarterback George Mira made the play of the game when his former high school teammate, UF defensive end Sam Holland,

---

[1]Associated Press, "Miami Hires Charles Tate," *Sarasota Herald-Tribune*, December 24, 1963.

[2]Associated Press, "Gators Have Best Season Since 1929," *St. Petersburg Evening Independent*, November 28, 1960.

grabbed his right arm and was about to drag him down. Mira managed to throw the ball left-handed for a spectacular fourth-quarter touchdown pass that sealed the victory.

That was the only losing season Florida suffered under Graves, who had his team pointed toward its second Gator Bowl appearance in three years in '62. The Gotham Bowl-bound Hurricanes sent them to that game licking their wounds when Bobby Wilson's 20-yard field goal in the fourth quarter gave Miami the 17–15 home triumph. The Gators had a chance to pull it out late, but UM's Bob Hart intercepted a Tom Shannon pass near midfield with less than a minute remaining. That '62 season was the first in which both Florida and Miami reached bowl games.

With expectations elevated, the Gators finally beat a Mira-led Miami attack in '63. The game took place the day after President John F. Kennedy was assassinated, and was thus an afterthought in the news of the day. Looking back, though, it can be considered one of the classic contests in the rivalry—a thrilling win for the Gators after dropping the previous two games in the series, and a bitter defeat that left Miami's Mira tearful in the locker room. "This is the worst one," he said after the 27–21 loss. "The most bitter defeat I've ever known as a football player."[3]

---

[3]Tom Kelly, "Pride Carried Gators, Hurricanes to 'Classic'," *St. Petersburg Times*, November 25, 1963.

There was talk that the City of Miami might not allow the Orange Bowl to be opened for the game while the nation mourned the loss of President Kennedy. UM President Dr. Henry King Stanford was granted his wish, though, and more than 57,000 fans showed up. "We are all aware of the President's great interest in sports and do not feel that the playing of the game can be accepted in any way as disrespect," Stanford said.[4]

Mira was brilliant in his first loss to the Gators, throwing three touchdown passes to account for all the Hurricane scoring. It was a pair of Miami natives who sparked Florida to victory. Tom Shannon directed a potent attack and produced two touchdowns on quarterback sneaks. And Hagood Clarke, protecting an injured ankle wearing high-top shoes, made his lone carry count. He took the ball on a fourth-quarter reverse play and broke loose for a 70-yard touchdown that gave the Gators the lead for good.

It didn't get any easier for Gustafson in his final season at Miami. Top 10 opponents Pittsburgh and Alabama rounded out the season, sending Mira and the Hurricanes home on a four-game losing streak. Enter Tate. The Florida grad was tasked with picking up the pieces of a 3–7 campaign, and with finding a way to lift Miami past his alma mater in the chase for state supremacy.

---

[4]Ibid.

It was not to be in 1964, although the underdog Hurricanes gave it a great run. Tate's opportunistic defense held Florida scoreless in the first half. A downpour contributed, too, as the Gators fumbled four times while allowing the Hurricanes to nab a 10–0 halftime lead. Sophomore quarterback Steve Spurrier, though, engineered two second-half touchdown drives to lift the Gators to a 12–10 victory. The winning score came when Larry Dupree hammered up the middle for 11 tough yards and a touchdown.

That would be the only time Spurrier would defeat Miami as a varsity player, as Tate and the Hurricanes were about to go on a run of three straight wins against their bitter rivals from up north.

Miami was just 5–4–1 in 1965, while Florida made the Sugar Bowl. However, that doesn't do justice to how strong Tate's Hurricanes were by the end of the season. They were the only team in college football to face Syracuse, Florida, and Notre Dame when all three were ranked in the Top 10. They were unbeaten (2–0–1) in those games, including a 16–13 upset of the Gators in November.

Florida dominated the first half at the Orange Bowl, racking up more than 200 yards before the intermission. The Gators led just 13–6 at halftime, though, a precarious edge. Sure enough, Miami came roaring back, inflicting its will with a powerful, between-the-tackles rushing attack. While the Florida offense struggled, determined backs Pete Banaszak and Doug McGee carried the Canes to 10 unanswered points and the win. "I felt all along we could run against them—shove it down their throats, if you want to be blunt about it," Tate said.[5]

"We should have stopped them in the second half, but we didn't," lamented Graves, who was fast becoming the target of scrutiny in Gainesville despite accepting a Sugar Bowl invitation after the game. "They were a lot of football team that second half. We didn't have the ball much and, when we did, we couldn't seem to get it going."[6]

The following year produced similar frustration for a strong Gator squad. Despite seven straight wins to open the '66 season, a 9–2 record, Top 10 ranking, Heisman Trophy honor by Spurrier and Orange Bowl victory over Georgia Tech—all hallmarks of a colossal year—another loss to the Hurricanes put at least a temporary pall on the celebration. Miami had rounded into one of the top teams in the country by the end of the season, going 7–0–1 in its last eight games (including a Liberty Bowl triumph over Virginia Tech).

The Hurricanes charged to a 21–3 advantage before withstanding a furious comeback attempt by Spurrier and the Gators. The game also featured some of the venom that had come to typify the rivalry. The Hurricanes took several shots at Spurrier, and the Gator quarterback called the officials "gutless"

---

[5]Associated Press, "Awkward Moment: Gators Meet Sugar Bowl Prexy," *Daytona Beach Morning Journal*, November 22, 1965.
[6]Ibid.

"The Ol' Ball Coach" Steve Spurrier first became a Florida legend as a young quarterback. In just three years, he passed for nearly 5,000 yards and 37 touchdowns, setting numerous school records and winning the 1966 Heisman Trophy. *AP Photo*

for not calling any roughing the passer penalties.[7] Tate accused the same referees of "lacking courage" for not penalizing Spurrier for intentional grounding as Florida stopped the clock in the final minute.[8] And the Gators were incensed by a fumble recovery the referees awarded to Miami that Florida end Paul Ewaldsen appeared to corral. In any event, Spurrier's last regular-season game ended in the arms of All-American Ted Hendricks, whose sack stopped the last UF drive.

Spurrier had graduated by the time the teams met again in 1967, and the Gators sure could have used him. Hendricks and the Hurricanes forced five Florida interceptions and recovered two fumbles to win by a 20–13 count at the Orange Bowl. Linebacker Ken Corbin returned two interceptions for touchdowns and Miami set up its other score

---

[7]Tom Kelly, "Gators, Tech Happy with Season Records," *St. Petersburg Times*, November 28, 1966.

[8]Ibid.

with Jimmy Dye's 79-yard punt return in beating the Gators for the third straight time.

Corbin had earned the nickname "Board Hands" earlier in his career for his inability to secure interceptions. "I guess we'll have to change that, won't we?" said Tate after the victory, which helped his team reach the Bluebonnet Bowl.[9]

The Hurricanes were favored to make it four in a row against the Gators in 1968 and took a 10–0 lead at halftime, but UF running back Larry Smith would have none of it. After helping the Gators climb within 10–7 late in the game, he made the final carry of his college career a memorable one.

Smith took a handoff at the Miami 6-yard line, was stuffed at the line of scrimmage and bounced the run to the outside. Two Miami defenders jumped on him at the 2, but the powerful back carried them into the end zone with 2:38 remaining as Florida rallied to win at home, 14–10.

"That was one of the greatest plays of a great career," said Graves, whose team claimed the state championship on the strength of that victory and an earlier win over Florida State. "Larry simply said, 'I want in that end zone more than you want to keep me out.' He played hurt all year

---

[9]Roger Bear, "The Clock Ran Out," *Daytona Beach Morning Journal*, December 10, 1967.

and nobody could have faulted him if he had decided to save himself for pro football, but he gave us 200 percent all the time."[10]

Florida-Miami in the 1960s

Date	Location	Winner	Score
November 26, 1960	Miami, FL	Florida	18–0
December 2, 1961	Gainesville, FL	Miami	15–6
December 1, 1962	Miami, FL	Miami	17–15
November 23, 1963	Miami, FL	Florida	27–21
November 28, 1964	Gainesville, FL	Florida	12–10
November 20, 1965	Miami, FL	Miami	16–13
November 26, 1966	Gainesville, FL	Miami	21–16
December 9, 1967	Miami, FL	Miami	20–13
November 30, 1968	Gainesville, FL	Florida	14–10
November 29, 1969	Miami, FL	Florida	35–16

[10]Tom Kelly, "Gators' Graves Enters Recruiting Wars As 'No. 1'," *St. Petersburg Times*, December 2, 1968.

9

GUSTAFSON SHIFTS MIAMI INTO "DRIVE"

FOR A MAN who was known to ride a bicycle to work often during his coaching career to keep his big body in shape, Andy Gustafson made his greatest headway with the word "drive." It was engrained in him as a star running back, and he preached it constantly to his players once he started coaching. He credited it for perhaps the greatest win of his coaching career—a 20–14 Miami upset at Purdue in 1950.

"Drive," Gustafson noted following the win against a Boilermakers team that had just ended Notre Dame's 39-game unbeaten streak the week before. "That's what did it. Drive, drive, and more drive. I got the idea when I was fullback at Aurora High School (in Illinois). The coach never let the backfield forget the idea it was supposed to hit hard. He had the word 'drive' printed on the back of every lineman's shirt, so we'd be thinking about it on every play."[1]

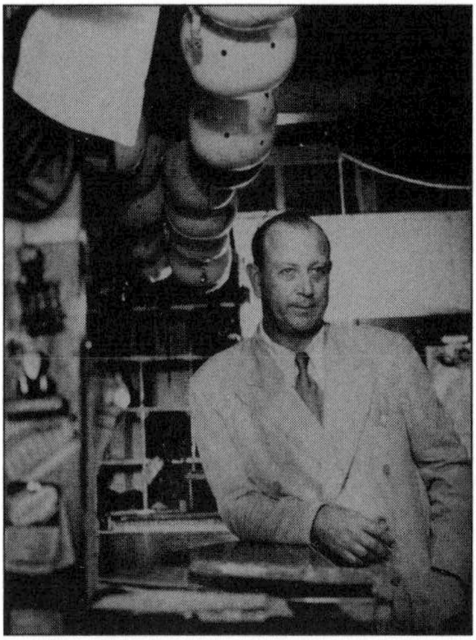

Known for an option play that would later grow in popularity as the veer and wishbone, Andy Gustafson took a Miami program that had only once appeared in a bowl game to four of them. His 9–7 record against Florida makes him the winningest head-to-head coach in the series. *1950 Miami Ibis via Wikimedia Commons*

Gustafson's "Drive Series" belly option play was considered an early version of the veer and wishbone offenses. The run-heavy attack, and his drive, served Gustafson well throughout his Hall of Fame career as both player and coach. He was a backfield mate of his Miami coaching predecessor, Jack Harding, while starring collegiately in legendary coach Glenn "Pop" Warner's Pittsburgh backfield. Gustafson holds the distinction of having scored the very first touchdown in Pitt Stadium on a run against Washington & Lee in 1925.

His passion and understanding of the game earned him a head coaching job right out of college. Gustafson coached

[1]United Press International, "Andy Gustafson Wins United Press Nod as Coach of the Week," *Reading Eagle*, October 18, 1950.

Virginia Tech to a 22–13–1 mark in four seasons at the helm before returning to Pitt as backfield coach under Jock Sutherland. In 1934, he hooked up with another revered head coach in Earl "Red" Blaik. Gustafson assisted Blaik first at Dartmouth and later at Army, where he coached the incomparable backfield of Glenn Davis and Doc Blanchard on one of most formidable juggernauts in college football history.

When Harding gave up the Miami coaching job to become athletic director at the school in 1947, Gustafson was not among the applicants for the job. He was enjoying his gig coaching backfield stars at a national powerhouse. However, he was the only candidate Harding was interested in. Harding reached out to his former Pittsburgh backfield mate, and Gustafson stepped up to the challenge.

Following Harding would be no easy task. The winningest coach in school history to that point had posted four seasons with eight or more wins in his nine-year tenure and captured the Orange Bowl to cap a 9–1–1 showing in 1945. However, nine years into his own 16-year tenure at the Hurricanes' helm, Gustafson also owned four eight-win seasons, had topped Harding's career victory total to become Miami's career leader, and had led UM to an Orange Bowl appearance and Gator Bowl victory.

Gustafson believed in hard work, hard running, and a hard-hitting defense. His no-nonsense approach called for his Hurricanes to be the tougher, more strong-willed team every time they took the field. And the approach produced results.

Over 16 seasons, he won 93 games against 65 losses and three ties. His teams made four bowl appearances–three more than Miami had ever earned before he arrived. Five UM teams cracked the Associated Press Top 10 rankings under his watch.

Though he demanded a lot from his players and coaching staff, Gustafson was also a well-liked man, great with fans and the media, and often ready with a quick quip or insightful quote. Before leading the Hurricanes against mighty Alabama in 1952, Gustafson accidentally walked into the branch of an orange tree in his yard and scratched the cornea of his left eye. Addressing the fact he was going to wear an eye patch for the game, the head coach joked, "I'll probably see too much of that Alabama team even with one eye."[2]

While the win at Purdue in 1950 probably stands as his greatest upset, he also led Miami to signature victories over Navy, Notre Dame, Alabama, Penn State, Iowa, Missouri, Michigan State, and other national powers.

One of Gustafson's most lasting accomplishments as Miami head coach involved not a national power, but a fledgling in-state school looking to establish itself. Florida State, an all-girls college until 1947, had been trying to get on the schedules of other state schools. "We are always anxious to

---

[2]Associated Press, "Andy Gustafson Walks into Tree; Hurts Eye," *Sarasota Herald-Tribune*, October 3, 1952.

play other schools in the state," Gustafson said. "If FSU can't get the Gators, they may like to play us."[3]

So Harding and Gustafson put the Seminoles on the schedule for a 1951 game at the Orange Bowl, beginning a rivalry that would grow to be the biggest on the Hurricanes' slate. Florida State and Florida did not get together until 1958.

Like Harding before him, Gustafson eventually gave up his coaching duties to focus solely on serving Miami as athletic director. He announced the decision in March of 1963, but coached the football team that fall before hiring Charlie Tate, a Florida grad, as his replacement. And like Harding before him, his final slate was one that didn't match expectations—a 3–7 slate that ended a string of four straight winning seasons and back-to-back bowl appearances.

Gustafson led UM sports as athletic director until 1968. Four years later, he was inducted in the University of Miami Sports Hall of Fame. He died at age seventy-five in 1979, six years before his posthumous induction into the College Football Hall of Fame.

Gustafson once told a story about a man who approached him on the street and asked if he had any money. "No," he replied, "but I've got memories that are worth millions."[4]

---

[3]Michael Bradley, *Big Games: College Football's Greatest Rivalries* (Washington: Potomac Books, 2006), 44.

[4]Associated Press, "Andy Gustafson Dead at 75," *Sumter Daily Item*, January 8, 1979.

The Gustafson File

Name: Andrew Gustafson

Born: April 3, 1903, Aurora, Illinois

Died: January 7, 1979, Coral Gables, Florida

Playing career: University of Pittsburgh (1923–25)

Head coaching career: Virginia Tech (1926–29), University of Miami (1948–63)

Athletic director: University of Miami (1963–68)

10

GRAVES BREATHES LIFE INTO GATORS

RAY GRAVES, IT can be argued, did more for the University of Florida's football program than anyone not named Steve Spurrier. And because it was Graves who recruited and mentored Spurrier, the Gators' only Heisman Trophy winner, who went on to coach two national championship teams, it can be contended without great resistance that Graves might actually eclipse his top pupil for impact.

Wherever he ranks among the all-time UF legends, one thing is certain. Graves was precisely the man the Gators needed when searching for a head coach and athletic director before the 1960 season. They found him coaching defense for the legendary Bobby Dodd at Georgia Tech, where he had made a name for himself with several schematic innovations that helped the Yellow Jackets to a pair of Southeastern Conference championships and a national title (1952) in the '50s.

There could hardly have been a more stark personality change when Graves replaced Bob Woodruff atop the Florida program. While Woodruff had been a quiet, conservative leader who rarely said much, Graves was the polar opposite. Gregarious and outspoken, he was a reporter's dream and fan favorite from the moment he arrived. His players loved him, too.

"He is a refreshing personality, full of parlor polish and the social graces, direct and frank, articulate and earnest," wrote *Daytona Beach Morning Journal* sports editor Bernard Kahn during Graves's first year in Gainesville. "You won't find a better salesman among the business executives, doctors and lawyers who populate the Q.B. Club membership than Ray Graves, son of a Knoxville, Tenn., Methodist minister."[1]

Of course, smooth talk and social graces don't win football games like they do elections, so Graves still had his work cut out for him at the helm of a program that had not won more than six games since '52. Woodruff had given Florida fans a taste of success, including the program's first bowl victory, but the Gators had stalled in the "good, not great" category. Graves was hired to change that.

The Tennessee native, who enjoyed a brief career as a center in the NFL before focusing on the coaching ranks, got right to work. "It takes at least two touchdowns to win

---

[1]Bernard Kahn, "Graves Wins Games and Respect as New Coach," *Daytona Beach Morning Journal*, November 20, 1960.

most college games," Graves said during his debut season. "I've told my boys we'll operate on a theory we're behind 12–0 at the start. With that philosophy, we gamble a little more but it doesn't keep us from playing smart football."[2]

The approach worked well from the outset. Graves's first team, in 1960, lost just twice—10–0 to Rice and 10–7 to Auburn. The Gators won nine times, scoring at least 12 points in every victory but a 3–0 nail-biter over Florida State. Their second-place SEC finish was their best ever, and they capped the year with a 13–12 Gator Bowl triumph against Baylor. It was just the second bowl win in school history.

Graves would go on to win all three Gator Bowl games he coached in, but that first was the most thrilling. Don Goodman ran for one touchdown and Larry Travis recovered a Baylor fumble in the end zone to give Florida the lead. The Bears' Ronnie Stanley, however, was one of the hottest quarterbacks in the country and led his team to two fourth-quarter touchdowns. His 47-yard toss to Ronnie Goodwin set up a short TD to make the score 13–12 in the late moments. Having missed an extra-point kick earlier, the Bears decided to go for two points and the win rather than kicking for the tie. Stanley's last pass hit Goodwin in the hands, but the ball was juggled and fell to the grass, allowing UF to prevail in dramatic fashion. It was quite a gift on Graves's forty-second

[2]Ibid.

birthday. He called it his "greatest relief"[3] upon his 1989 induction into the Gator Bowl Hall of Fame.

With that opening season, the Graves era was off and running. Florida fans were ecstatic. "The school and its followers can look forward to a golden era in the game," wrote Bob Boyson of the *St. Petersburg Evening Independent*. "They can hang the 'patsy' handle on somebody else—the Southeastern Conference's coach of the year will be far too busy to take the time it requires to pick it up."[4]

It wasn't all smooth sailing from there. Graves experienced some growing pains, stumbling to 4–5–1 in 1961. As his system took hold, however, so did the Gators' success. They never again had a losing record under his watch and won at least seven games in four of the next five seasons. They beat Penn State, 17–7, in the 1962 Gator Bowl, cracked the AP Top 10 for the first time ever in '64, and lost a two-point decision to Missouri the following season with a junior standout named Spurrier playing quarterback.

Despite losing their top two receivers entering '66, Graves and Spurrier enjoyed their best season together. Their only losses in a 9–2 campaign came against Georgia and Miami in November, but the Gators still earned an Orange Bowl berth

---

[3]Norm Froscher, "Former Head Gator's in Gator Bowl Hall of Fame," *Gainesville Sun*, September 19, 1989.

[4]Bob Boyson, "Florida's Family Finish Best in School's History," *St. Petersburg Evening Independent*, November 29, 1960.

against Georgia Tech. At the time, Graves called the 27–12 drubbing of the Yellow Jackets the greatest win of his career.

Consecutive six-win seasons followed before Graves closed his Florida career with another banner campaign in '69. The Gators set the tone in the opening game by drubbing seventh-ranked Houston, 59–34. It was their first of six straight wins to start the season. A loss to Auburn and a tie with Georgia the next two weeks provided the only blemishes on a 9–1–1 campaign that culminated with a 35–16 rout over Miami and a thrilling 14–13 win over Tennessee in the Gator Bowl.

Florida coach Ray Graves, pictured here during a 1969 victory over Miami, brought both personality and success to the Gators in the 1960s. His five wins against the Hurricanes rank him third—behind only Andy Gustafson and Doug Dickey—among coaches with the most wins in the series. *AP Photo*

With a 70–31–4 record, Graves announced that he was giving up his coaching position to focus solely on the AD portion of his job. Moments after the announcement reached the ears of his players, his bosses, and Gators fans everywhere, Doug Dickey's name started surfacing as the logical replacement. Graves endorsed hiring the former UF star, too, and so it came to be.

In January of 1979, Graves gave up the AD post as well, saying he and wife Opal had decided on his sixtieth birthday several days earlier it was time to retire. He dedicated himself to fundraising for the university thereafter, his heart never leaving the Gators. He also served as an advisor to colorful and controversial New York Yankees owner George Steinbrenner. Graves died at age ninety-six in 2015, but not before several of his friends, colleagues, and former players said farewell.

"A tremendous influence on my life," Spurrier said of Graves, a 1990 inductee into the College Football Hall of Fame. "After my mother and dad, Coach Graves had the biggest influence on my life. I am so thankful for him. I had a chance yesterday to tell him I love him and I sincerely thank him for the influence he had on me."[5]

---

[5]Jerry Hinnen, "Former Florida Coach, AD Ray Graves Dies at 96," *CBS Sports*, April 10, 2015.

The Graves File

Name: Samuel Ray Graves
Born: December 31, 1918, Knoxville, Tennessee
Died: April 10, 2015, Clearwater, Florida
Playing career: University of Tennessee (1940–41), Philadelphia Eagles (1942–43, 1946)
Head coaching career: University of Florida (1960–69)
Athletic director: University of Florida (1960–79)

11

"CUBAN COMET" LIGHTS UP MIAMI

MIAMI WAS MORE than a home to Carlos Alvarez and his family. It was a safe haven. The Alvarez family had fled there from Cuba in 1960, when Carlos was ten and Fidel Castro was rising to power after a communist revolution. Carlos's father, Licinio, had been a successful attorney in their homeland but knew that coming to America would give his family a better chance to thrive. He had no idea what success might be in store for his son, or the impact the family move would have on Florida football.

Though baseball and soccer far surpassed American football for popularity in Cuba, Carlos found himself enjoying the gridiron at North Miami Senior High School. He was a smart, quick, sure-handed halfback who also stood out in the defensive secondary. It was not uncommon for Alvarez to play all forty-eight minutes of his high school games. His talent did not go unnoticed. In addition to earning several Dade County honors as one of the best players in the area, he was recruited by several Division I colleges. Both Florida and hometown Miami were among them. Carlos chose the Gators.

It was a decision he never regretted. "I enjoyed playing college athletics and I really enjoyed my four years at the University of Florida," he noted. "I know people say it a lot, but I wouldn't change that time for the world."[1]

It was not always easy, but any difficulty was largely Alvarez's own doing. The "Cuban Comet," playing for head coach Ray Graves, was one of the first players at Florida to emphasize the value of year-round work. Few toiled harder than Carlos did on the field, in the workout room, or in the classroom. The three-time Academic All-American also inspired many of his teammates and classmates to follow suit.

"I felt that if you want to present the best product, you couldn't stop working at it," he said. "That's one of the things that really helped me at Florida."[2]

It was bad enough for Miami that Alvarez chose to attend college in Gainesville. That he plied his trade *against* his hometown school was almost too much to bear. That was

[1]Pat Dooley, "Florida's Alvarez Elected to College Hall of Fame," *Gainesville Sun*, May 17, 2011.

[2]Kelly Reynolds, "Carlos Alvarez—Walk Proud," *University of Florida Communications*, September 29, 2008.

never more true, or painful, for the Hurricanes than when he and his fellow "Super Sophs"—a crew of talented sophomores that featured John Reaves, Tommy Durrance, and Jack Youngblood—paid a visit to the Orange Bowl in November of 1969. It was Carlos's first hometown return, and it turned into a homecoming for the ages.

Alvarez simply could not be covered. He raced around the Miami secondary as if the Gators were running passing drills, catching 15 passes for 237 yards. Both set school records. Two of his receptions went for touchdowns as the Gators, on their way to a 9–1–1 record and Gator Bowl championship, thrashed the rival Hurricanes by a 35–16 score.

Carlos Alvarez left home in Miami to play football in Gainesville, and the Hurricanes wound up kicking themselves for letting him get away. The Cuban-born receiver set records with 15 catches for 237 yards and added two touchdowns in a 1969 Florida win over Miami at the Orange Bowl. *AP Photo*

"I was the first Cuban to really play football," Alvarez recalled years later, "so going back to the Orange Bowl was great. They packed the place and it was mostly people cheering for Florida. The last pass, they put me in to score one more touchdown for all of the Cubans who had come to the game. They put me in the slot so a safety would be covering me and it worked."[3]

Almost everything UF did that day worked, with perhaps one exception. Alvarez beat a defender deep on a fly pattern from his own 1-yard line late in the game, but Reaves's pass was slightly underthrown. It fell incomplete, or Carlos might have topped 300 receiving yards.

His single-game records for receptions and yardage were hardly the only marks to fall. Alvarez also broke SEC single-season records for receptions, yards, and touchdowns in that game. Reaves, meanwhile, completed 30 of 43 passes for 346 yards, and his 24th touchdown pass broke a nineteen-year-old SEC record. Durrance rushed for three touchdowns.

Alvarez set other Florida receiving records, including the career receptions mark of 172. The Dallas Cowboys drafted him after he graduated with a degree in political science in 1972, but chronic knee problems and a desire to follow in the footsteps of his father and older brothers steered him toward Duke University School of Law instead of the NFL. Carlos enjoyed a successful career as an attorney, mainly in Tallahassee. He made the drive from there to Gainesville in 2007 to watch his UF career receiving mark fall, after thirty-eight years, to Andre "Bubba" Caldwell.

---

[3]Pat Dooley, "It's Time '84, '85, '90 Honors Brought Down," *Gainesville Sun*, September 5, 2002.

"I'm thrilled for him," Alvarez said. "I really am. He's such a nice kid."[4]

In 2002, Taylor Jacobs broke the single-game receiving yardage record Alvarez set against Miami. His 15 catches in a game, however, still stood atop the Gator record book entering the 2016 season, as did his 88 receptions in a season and 2,563 career receiving yards. Not bad for a kid with bad knees.

In 2011, the "Comet" was caught off guard by an even more prestigious honor. He was informed he was being inducted into the College Football Hall of Fame.

"I'm really honored," he said. "Anybody who knows anything about college football knows there are plenty of players who should be in there. Why you end up making it is a bit of a guess."[5]

Added then-Florida coach Will Muschamp, "Growing up a Gator fan, I was very aware of what Carlos accomplished, setting most of the receiving records in an era when you could only play three years and the seasons were only 11 games long. Carlos was equally successful in the classroom at UF and he has carried that success to his law practice."[6]

Two years after his record-setting day, Alvarez enjoyed another trip home with a 45–16 Gator romp in his second and final game at the Orange Bowl. Miami was very good to him, indeed.

---

[4]Reynolds, "Carlos Alvarez."

[5]Pat Dooley, "Florida's Alvarez Elected to College Hall of Fame," *Gainesville Sun*, May 17, 2011.

[6]Ibid.

The Alvarez File

Name: Carlos Alvarez Vasquez Rodriguez Ubieta
Born: April 1, 1950, Havana, Cuba
Records set at Florida include: Receptions in a game (15), season (88), and career (172); receiving yards in a game (237), season (1,329), and career (2,563); touchdown receptions in a season (12); and consecutive games with a reception (25).
Highlights: First college reception went for a 70-yard touchdown against Houston . . . Led the NCAA in 1969 in receptions, receiving yards, touchdown receptions and total yards from scrimmage . . . Caught the pass that gave John Reaves the NCAA career passing yardage record ... Became the youngest player to make the AFCA All-America team ... Three-time Academic All-American and member of the Academic All-America Hall of Fame . . . 2011 College Football Hall of Fame inductee.

12

FLOP GOES THE RIVALRY

"THE FLOP." IT'S all one needs to say to get longtime Miami Hurricanes fans riled up. One play, the Gator Flop, did more to stoke the flames of the Florida-Miami rivalry than any late hit, verbal taunt, or dramatic victory. "Totally reprehensible," said Howard Schnellenberger, who was an assistant coach with the Miami Dolphins at the time and would go on to take the Hurricanes to new heights eight years later. "Bush league" was the description given by then-Hurricanes coach Fran Curci, whose team received a "free" touchdown out of it.

Let's start at the beginning. Curci had been coaching at the University of Tampa fourteen months before the Gator Flop, and had called the Florida Gators "crybabies" in the press. When he was tabbed to coach the Hurricanes in 1971, he understood that a November 27 visit by Florida to the

Orange Bowl would loom large on the Gators' calendar. He had no idea just how large.

Florida's accomplished senior class included quarterback John Reaves, who wound up trailing Jim Plunkett by 343 yards for the all-time NCAA passing yardage record entering that final regular-season date. Reaves was already filled with motivation, knowing about the Miami coach's comments of the previous year. "We are coming down here to teach Fran Curci a lesson," Reaves said.[1] Now, with a chance to make college football history on the line, Reaves was truly a man on a mission.

Throwing for 350 yards in a college football game was a longshot at that time, before spread offenses and no-huddle attacks became commonplace. Reaves, however, came out firing. He led Florida to a 17–0 halftime lead and was almost midway to the needed yardage, with 170 passing yards. The Gators were blowing out the Hurricanes by the fourth quarter, and Reaves was within 12 yards of the mark.

Florida lined up to field a Miami punt late in the game, and Gators head coach Doug Dickey was getting his aerial plays ready for Reaves to break the record. Just one small problem: UF return man Harvin Clark broke loose and returned the punt for a touchdown. He immediately ran to the sideline and apologized to his coaches and teammates.

---

[1]Bruce Lowitt, "1971: Just for the Record, Gators Did Their Famous Flop," *St. Petersburg Times*, September 2, 1986.

"After I crossed the goal line, I thought, 'Aw, hell,'" Clark recalled. "And I went over to John and I said, 'John, I think I screwed this thing up for you.' He said, 'Aw, don't worry about it.'"[2]

"We've laughed many a time—John, Harvin and I—about that," Dickey noted. "All he had to do was fall down. We didn't need the touchdown. Just give us the ball! But we don't get the ball, we get seven points."

Now Miami had the ball and began to march down the field with its wishbone offense. Florida called timeouts in hopes of stopping the Hurricanes and giving Reaves one more chance. Once those timeouts were gone, however, there was only one way to regain possession of the ball without a turnover. The UF players started hounding Dickey to let Miami score a touchdown. The crowd began chanting, "Let them score! Let them score!" Finally, with 1:20 on the clock and the Hurricanes at Florida's 7-yard line, the head coach instructed his defense to do just that.

"I felt like I owed it to John to do something to help him out," Dickey said. "He'd had a great career and I felt like I owed John that opportunity."

Dickey said after the game that he didn't expect the surrender to be so dramatic. As soon as Miami snapped the ball, most of the Gators fell to their stomachs at

---

[2]Paul Lukas "The Stories Behind the 1971 Gator Flop," ESPN.com, September 16, 2010.

the line of scrimmage, allowing quarterback John Hornibrook to run uncontested into the end zone. The Flop was born.

"I never thought they'd do it the way they did," Dickey said. "We have many practice plays where we brush but don't tackle. I thought they'd do that."[3]

The game that might have done the most to fuel the Florida-Miami rivalry was the 1971 "Gator Flop" contest that resulted in John Reaves setting the NCAA career record for passing yardage. The star Gators quarterback got the opportunity he needed when his teammates let Miami score in the late going. *AP Photo*

Reaves almost rendered the gesture moot when he was nearly picked off on first down. He then hit star receiver Carlos Alvarez for 15 yards to pass Plunkett's 7,544 career passing yards. Reaves left the game, mostly to cheers, and then returned for one more short completion just in case the stat keepers were a bit off in their math. He finished with 348 passing yards and a 45–16 victory.

"I was appalled," Curci said. "I just couldn't believe it. I thought this was so much against the spirit of the game that I came back out later and

[3]Lowitt, "1971."

said it was a tainted record. I was very, very angry. My players, they were just incensed. A couple of 'em were crying."[4]

"I found it no different from an intentional pass in baseball or a late-game basketball decision to let a man shoot to regain possession, or intentionally fouling," Dickey said. "We did not do it because it was Miami or Curci. We did it for John and for our team."[5]

Two Gators, most notably John Clifford, did not drop to the ground on the play. Clifford was actually in position to make the tackle but allowed Hornibrook to run past him.

"I took the gratuitous Catholic genuflect," Clifford said. "So I can't be considered any better than anyone else out there. And when John Hornibrook ran past me, he had the most disgusting look on his face I had ever seen. He was definitely not happy. And I was embarrassed. I was."[6]

"When they all fell down," Miami's Chuck Foreman said, "we were all just, 'What the heck is this?' At the moment, I was in shock because I didn't even understand what was going on, to be honest with you. But once it set in, I'm like, 'Man, this is the worst thing I've ever heard of or seen in a football game.'"[7]

---

[4]Paul Lukas, "The Stories."

[5]Lowitt, "1971."

[6]Lukas, "The Stories."

[7]Ibid.

What the Gators did next added insult to, well, insult. After the game, UF players raced to the fountain beyond the end zone in the Orange Bowl and jumped in, splashing around in celebration. The gesture was not lost on the Hurricanes, many of whom vowed revenge.

"Going in the fountain? That's rubbing it in worse than I rubbed it in," Schnellenberger said in 2015, referring to a time he was accused of running up the score against the Gators with a late field goal.

"I had a Miami fan accost me in the parking lot a few years ago over the Flop," said *Gainesville Sun* writer Pat Dooley, a veteran beat writer covering the Gators. "I'm like, 'Dude, I didn't flop. I wasn't even there.' But that is, to me, one of the funniest moments in the history of sports. And that they took it personally . . . you know, I can get that . . . but it almost makes it even funnier.

"I remember the next year in Gainesville, Miami students were passing out these cards. And I can't even remember what they said, but it was something about the Flop and classless Florida. Fran Curci, on his death bed, his last word will be 'Flop.'"

13

ONE FOR THE BIRDS . . . AND GATORS

WISE MONEY WOULD be on the strong-jawed reptile in any matchup between thin marsh bird and giant alligator. Make it two gators versus one bird, and no odds-maker would take the bet.

However, this is a story about a football rivalry in Florida, a state renowned for offbeat news and the unexpected. So when it comes to college football mascots, nothing should come as a surprise—not even a skinny bird getting under the skin of an alligator or two. Namely, UF mascots Albert and Alberta Gator.

"That little duck they got," said former Florida star Ben Troupe, referring to the University of Miami's mascot, Sebastian the Ibis, "he's like a trained serial killer. In the Sugar Bowl [in 2001], I remember that duck beating up Albert [Florida's mascot]. I was like, 'Albert, fight back, man! We're already losing the game.'"

For the record, Sebastian is not a duck. He's an ibis, a bird that represents knowledge in ancient folklore and can be found in the Florida Everglades. The UM yearbook chose the name "Ibis" in 1926, swayed by the bravery of the bird. It's known to be the last wildlife creature to take shelter in a hurricane, and the first to emerge after a storm. Thus began its run as unofficial school mascot.

Sebastian the Ibis became the official school mascot shortly after a dorm, San Sebastian Hall, entered an ibis in a 1957 Homecoming celebration. The next year, student John Stormont dressed as the bird and entertained fans during a home football game, beginning a most interesting study in character development.

Over the years, Sebastian's role has evolved with a couple of exceptions that some might describe as "devolution."

The job has been held by a Miami student for the most part, except for a stretch from 1984 to '92 when it was in the hands of a full-time employee. It was during that period when John Routh, a veteran Sebastian who was looking to push the boundaries of a good prank—all in good fun, of course—wore fireman's gear and carried a fire extinguisher in Tallahassee in 1989 with plans to feign extinguishing Florida State's mascot's flaming spear. The previous two trips to Tallahassee, Routh had gotten a reaction by "threatening" to put out Chief Osceola's flame with a bucket of water.

This time, he got more reaction than he bargained for when he was corralled by police officers before reaching the field.

"I heard someone yelling, 'Give me the effing fire extinguisher! Give it to me!'" Routh recalled. "And so I screamed, 'No!' But of course nobody could hear me because I'm in a bird costume. As I screamed, I jerked away from him and I just happened to squeeze the trigger [to the extinguisher], which splashed onto the chest of a Leon County officer and at that moment, I realized, 'Uh-oh, something is wrong here.'"[1]

Other officers quickly joined the scene and pinned Sebastian—er, Routh—against a fence. Routh said one of the officers indicated they were going to take him to jail and charge him with disorderly conduct and disobeying an officer until a UM cheerleading coach came and helped defuse the tension.

"Then they realized, this probably doesn't look good," Routh offered. "Five Leon Country police officers beating up a guy in a bird costume."[2]

While Sebastian's feisty side has matched his team's bravado well over the years, 99 percent of his performances are family friendly. The mascot who started as in-game entertainment now makes more than two hundred community appearances annually. Less than half of those are at games. Kids' parties, alumni events, local road races, and countless charity functions have all gone to the birds.

---

[1]Laken Litman, "24 Years Ago the Miami Hurricanes Mascot Was Detained Before the Florida State Game," *USA Today*, October 31, 2013.

[2]Ibid.

"I guess I have always been somewhat of a class clown throughout my life," said Joe Dorsey, who played Sebastian in the early 1970s, at a Sebastian the Ibis reunion held in 2005. "I probably should have been a game show host instead of a banker."[3]

When Sebastian and a pair of Gators get together, "family feud" comes to mind. That's because Albert E. and Alberta Gator have each other's hearts—and backs—when they appear together at UF games.

UF did not have an official mascot when the program started in 1906. Two years later, UF merchandise depicting alligators began showing up in the Gainesville shop of Phillip Miller and his son, Austin. The team started being referred to publicly as the Gators in 1911, and in 1957, a live alligator was first brought to the field as team mascot.

Fortunately for anyone a little unnerved by having an actual gator near the sideline, a costumed version appeared in 1970. Albert has since earned acclaim as one of the best and most recognized mascots in college football by no less authority than *Sports Illustrated* over the years, and Alberta came along in 1984 to double the entertainment value at The Swamp.

The look has changed significantly over the years, but perhaps the greatest evolution for both Albert and Alberta came recently. Before the 2015 season, the school debuted new, lighter costumes for its famed First Couple. The athletic

[3]Alumni Digest, "For the Birds," *Miami Magazine*, Fall 2005.

department described them as "much more lightweight and customized for [the] hot Florida weather."[4]

Whether performing the "Gator Chomp," reciting the famed "Two Bits" cheer (Two bits, four bits, six bits, a dollar! All for the Gators stand up and holler!), or entertaining at hundreds of community events in the Gainesville area, the lighter gear came as a welcome relief to Albert and Alberta.

After all, the easier it is to maneuver when there's a troublemaking ibis around, the better.

Both Schools' Mascots Crack Top 25

Sports Illustrated was enamored with college football in Florida when it announced its Top 25 College Football Mascots in 2015. Ibis ranked No. 12 in the rankings, with the magazine both raving and taking a dig at "The U." "Just like Puddles at Oregon," *SI* wrote, "only with more national championships and way more sanctions." Of twenty-fourth-ranked Albert and Alberta, it simply said: "Dawwwwwwwww. They're so cute."

Neither school could do a whole lot of in-state boasting, however, as Florida State's Chief Osceola was ranked No. 1.

[4]Andy Hutchins, "Florida Gators Mascots Albert, Alberta Getting New Costumes," *SB Nation*, July 17, 2015.

14

1970s: GATORS WIN SEVEN IN A ROW

FLORIDA VICTORIES OVER Miami were as regular as bell-bottom jeans, lava lamps, and disco music in the 1970s. The rivalry became one-sided during the decade, with the Gators winning seven games in a row between 1971 and '77 and pulling ahead in the all-time series for the first time since the 1940s.

Florida fans who recall Miami's upset win in 1970 are still scratching their heads over what could have been a 10-game winning streak dating to '68. The lone blemish was a shocker that cost UF a berth in the Liberty Bowl. Miami had lost six in a row entering the game in Gainesville, where all the heavily favored Gators had to do was win to secure a bowl date with Colorado. Against their biggest rival, though, the Hurricanes played their most inspired ball of the season.

They drove 70 yards on the game's opening possession and rode a Tom Sullivan plunge to a 7–0 advantage. In the third quarter, a two-yard touchdown sweep by Scott Mundrick gave Miami a 14–0 cushion and had 50,000-plus Florida fans eerily quiet at The Swamp. John Clifford's 50-yard return of an interception for a touchdown changed that, getting UF back in the game, and when John Reaves found Terry Ash for a 41-yard touchdown with 8:11 to go, it appeared the Gators would be bowling after all.

If not for shaky kicking, they would have. Jim Getzen, who had been perfect on extra points and field goals since taking over the job in midseason, missed one of each down the stretch. His missed PAT after the Ash touchdown kept Miami on top 14–13, and his missed 25-yard field goal try with 29 seconds remaining prevented the Gators from pulling out a dramatic victory.

It was the last loss Florida would suffer at the hands of Miami until 1978. The Gators' seven-game victory streak began with a flop—"The Flop"—documented in Chapter 12. While the finish to that 1971 game brought controversy, bitter feelings, and embarrassment, what should not be lost was the fact Florida won by 29 points despite allowing a Miami touchdown on purpose. The talent gap between the two rivals was widening. Florida went to four bowl games in the 1970s; Miami none.

The Gators' 17–6 home win in 1972 was hardly a thing of beauty. Players from both schools had professed to be champing at the bit to get after each other following the events of the previous fall, but you would not have known it from the caliber of play. Through three quarters, a field goal by Florida freshman John Williams accounted for the only points in front of a disappointing crowd of 46,000.

Two Gator touchdowns 46 seconds apart in the fourth quarter put the Hurricanes away. Nat Moore, who topped 100 rushing yards, burst 18 yards to the Miami 1-yard line and then capped the drive with a touchdown. On the ensuing UM possession, UF freshman Wayne Fields intercepted an Ed Carney pass and returned it for a touchdown to make it 17-0. The Hurricanes reached the end zone in the final minutes to avert the shutout.

Pete Elliott was in his first season as Miami coach in 1973, and his Hurricanes had faced a "murderer's row" of talented teams that year. Florida was one of several bowl-bound squads on their schedule, but Elliott's boys played the Gators tough at the Orange Bowl. UF flanker Joel Parker caught a 7-yard touchdown pass and set up his team's second score on a 29-yard reception as the Gators held off a fourth-quarter Miami charge for a 14–7 victory.

The Hurricanes scored on a 29-yard grab by Phil August in the final quarter and drove to the Florida 5-yard line in the game's final minute, but a late stand by the Gators stopped the potential trying drive with 33 seconds on the clock.

Elliott had no such luck keeping the game competitive the following year in Gainesville. Two of his best players,

Woody Thompson and Rubin Carter, were out of the lineup. Furthermore, a cold rain created a muddy Florida Field that turned out to be perfectly suited for Gator coach Doug Dickey's wishbone attack. Throw in the fact UF was bound for a Sugar Bowl clash with Nebraska, and it was an over-matched Miami team that suffered a 31–7 setback in 1974.

Quarterback Don Gaffney directed an offense that took advantage of great field position, starting eight drives at its own 40-yard line or better. The Gators slopped to a 17–0 halftime lead, even scoring when they recovered their own fumble in the end zone, and never relented.

Gaffney and the Gators had to work much harder for a win over Miami in 1975. Despite the fact Carl Selmer's first Hurricanes team was wrapping up the first of two straight eight-loss seasons, UM saved its very best for Gator Bowl-bound Florida. In fact, the Hurricanes carried play for most of the game, which was played before just 25,000 fans at the Orange Bowl.

Florida struck first on a blocked punt for a safety, and a Miami field goal made it a 3–2 score at halftime. Gaffney's QB sneak gave the Gators an 8–3 lead in the third quarter, but after being stopped on fourth down deep in UF territory, the Hurricanes got the ball back and took an 11–8 lead on a 35-yard, final-quarter TD run by Larry Cain. With time churning down, an upset seemed to be in the making.

That is, until Miami punted the ball to Henry Davis, who took the ball 63 yards for the winning touchdown with less than four minutes to play. An interception in the end zone by Robby Ball then killed a final UM drive with 1:21 remaining after the Hurricanes had marched to the UF 16-yard line.

Selmer was livid about two calls. One was a Florida fumble recovery in the second quarter that the Miami coach claimed was not a fumble. The other was Davis's winning score. Selmer insisted the Florida return man touched the ground with his knee when he fielded the punt, and therefore should have been marked down at the spot. "The officials missed a good game out there," Selmer offered. "Some of those calls were just crazy . . . I asked the official if Davis' knee touched the ground. The official just told me to get off the field."[1]

The hard feelings between the schools were evident in postgame player comments as well. Miami center George Demopoulos, for instance, surmised, "If we played Florida's schedule, we'd be 9–2, too. Especially in that sissy SEC, where even [Alabama coach] Bear Bryant is scared to play the Big Eight runner-up. What a league. What a joke.[2]

Selmer was feeling the heat and almost out the door by the time his Hurricanes got another shot at the Gators in 1976. The game was played in Orlando, where Florida was favored by both the crowd and the oddsmakers. It was a stifling defense

---

[1]John Valerino, "Officials Missed a Good Game—Selmer," *Lakeland Ledger*, November 30, 1975.

[2]Hubert Mizell, "In Attaining New Heights, Gators Dizzy," *St. Petersburg Times*, December 1, 1975.

that got the job done for the Gators, even scoring on a safety in a 19–10 win.

"It was our defensive team's finest hour," said Florida coach Dickey, who also got big offensive days from quarterback Jimmy Fisher (14 of 21 for 263 yards) and receiver Wes Chandler. "They gave us field position, forced turnovers and even scored for us on the safety. We had the best defensive half of the season in the second half of this game."[3]

Florida quarterback Jimmy Fisher (pictured) and receiver Wes Chandler were too much for Miami to handle in a 1976 game in Orlando. The Gators won, 19–10, as Fisher went 14 of 21 passing. *AP Photo/Phil Sandlin*

Lou Saban replaced Selmer as Miami coach in 1977, not knowing that he would be the fourth consecutive sideline boss to last just two seasons at the helm. He carried on another tradition by falling to Florida in his debut to the rivalry. Struggling to keep players on the roster and fans in the seats, UM dropped a 31–14 decision at the Orange Bowl.

---

[3]Wire reports, "Gators' Defense Has Its Day," *Boca Raton News*, November 29, 1976.

Terry LeCount directed a potent UF offense while receivers Chandler and Tony Stephens hauled in spectacular catches to make their quarterback's job look easy. One of Chandler's catches was being replayed near Saban in the postgame press conference, prompting the Miami coach to conclude, "They've got a lot of people like that. We'll get our share down the line."[4]

It turned out Saban needed just one year to lift the Hurricanes to an unexpected win over the Gators, ending their seven-game losing streak in the series. It came in Dickey's final game as UF coach. It turned out to be Saban's finale at UM as well. The Hurricanes, who had said they didn't want Dickey to go until they had a chance to beat him, scored 19 unanswered points in the second half to do just that, posting a 22–21 upset in Gainesville.

Florida, breaking the norm with all-blue uniforms, got touchdown passes by Timmy Groves to Cris Collinsworth and Stephens in the early going as they raced to a 21–3 halftime lead. "We were so flat," Saban said, "I didn't think we could come out of it. I told them I wasn't going to let them out of the locker room until they proved they could do the job. I just looked in their eyes and I think they knew I meant what I said. They came to play in the second half."[5]

---

[4]Mike Tierney, "Like McKay, Saban Is Determined—and Struggling," *St. Petersburg Times*, November 28, 1977.

[5]Joe Biddle, "Swan Song Turns into the Blues," *Daytona Beach Morning Journal*, December 3, 1978.

Ottis Anderson heard the challenge and met it square on, as the workhorse running back he was. He caught a 3-yard touchdown pass and ran 8 yards for the winning score in the fourth quarter. UF turnovers helped, too. The Gators lost three fumbles and threw a remarkable seven interceptions to send their longtime coach off on a disappointing note.

"Everyone was talking about Florida winning one for their old coach," Saban said. "I said to my players, 'I'm older than he is. Why don't you guys go out there and win one for me.' They did."[6]

It was new leadership on both sides that wrapped up the 1970s in Miami. Howard Schnellenberger's Hurricanes took care of Charley Pell's Gators, 30–24, sending Florida to its first winless season since 1946. The game was not as close as the final score might indicate. Freshman Jim Kelly threw for one touchdown and ran for another for the Hurricanes, who certainly had the lower hand against Florida in the 1970s but were heading into the '80s with momentum. No one could have predicted the meteoric rise that was coming.

---

[6]Ibid.

Florida-Miami in the 1970s

Date	Location	Winner	Score
November 28, 1970	Gainesville, FL	Miami	14–13
November 27, 1971	Miami, FL	Florida	45–16
December 2, 1972	Gainesville, FL	Florida	17–6
November 24, 1973	Miami, FL	Florida	14–7
November 30, 1974	Gainesville, FL	Florida	31–7
November 29, 1975	Miami, FL	Florida	15–11
November 27, 1976	Orlando, FL	Florida	19–10
November 26, 1977	Miami, FL	Florida	31–14
December 2, 1978	Gainesville, FL	Miami	22–21
December 1, 1979	Miami, FL	Miami	30–24

15

DICKEY HAD MIAMI'S NUMBER, IF NOT FLORIDA'S

THE QUEST FOR a Southeastern Conference championship brought Doug Dickey to the University of Florida before the 1970 season. The same quest brought UF to Tennessee that year to pluck Dickey as its head coach. So right from the start, everyone was on the same page. And for a while, it looked like the marriage between Dickey and his alma mater might be a lasting one.

The SEC title never materialized, which turned out to be a very big deal among Gators administrators, boosters, and alumni. It didn't matter that Dickey would eventually wind up in the College Football Hall of Fame, with the bulk of his credentials being compiled at Tennessee. It didn't matter that he won seven consecutive games against Miami in the state's oldest rivalry. It didn't matter that he once led UF to 19 consecutive home victories, although one fan did hold a sign thanking him for that achievement during his final game as Florida coach.

"I came to Florida to see if we could win an SEC title," Dickey said. "It just didn't work out."[1]

Born in South Dakota, Douglas Adair Dickey moved to Gainesville as a child. He stayed home to attend UF, where he made the football team as a walk-on defensive back. He moved to quarterback and was buried at seventh on the depth chart in 1951, but his hard work had him climbing quickly. What he lacked in passing ability he made up for in smarts. Coach Bob Woodruff loved his mind and his ability to manage a game. The Gators found themselves without a starting quarterback during the 1952 season, so Dickey—remarkably—got his chance. By season's end, he had led them to a win in the first NCAA bowl game in program history.

Dickey earned his coaching stripes as an assistant at Arkansas before taking over Tennessee's program in 1964. He claimed two SEC crowns with the Volunteers and was also responsible for the large, orange "T" on their helmets and the orange-and-white checkerboard end zone patterns that remain staples today. With rumors swirling that he would be hired to coach Florida following the 1969 slate, it turned out his final game was against his alma mater in that year's Gator Bowl. UF handed him a 14–13 loss in that

---

[1]Gene Frenette, "As Gators-Volunteers Game Nears, Doug Dickey Still Roots for Both," *Florida Times-Union*, September 24, 2015.

game, and then entrusted its own SEC title hopes to the coach it had vanquished.

"The heart of any successful football program is first to recruit the best players," Dickey told Florida fans after his hiring. "Then don't let yourself get outcoached. Next, be lucky. Luck is when preparation meets opportunity. We feel when we've done that, we may be lucky. Finally, you have to play good defense."[2]

Gators fans, generally high on Dickey in the early days, will tell you that he was outcoached a time or two. They will also vouch for his commitment to defense. In fact, some criticized that his run-and defense-oriented brand of football was too boring.

He would have been forgiven for that, certainly, had an SEC championship arrived. However, after a 7–4 opening salvo in 1970, Dickey's Gators went 9–12–1 over the next two years. A run of four consecutive bowl trips began in 1973, but Florida lost all four.

Dickey got close to an SEC title twice, only to be thwarted by Georgia both times. In 1975, the Gators were three minutes from sharing the crown with Alabama when Georgia pulled out a 10–7 win on a 80-yard trick play with three minutes to go. The next season, the Bulldogs rallied from a 14-point second-half deficit after Florida failed on a critical

---

[2]*Daytona Beach Morning Journal,* "Dickey Hopes to Give Gators Football Championship in SEC," May 30, 1970.

fourth-down decision by Dickey that came to be known as "Fourth and Dumb." Georgia won, 41–27, denying the Gators an outright SEC crown.

"Doug was a good coach and had a great mind to make a decision on what he thought was right," said longtime UF Sports Information Director Norm Carlson. "Other people might back off a controversial decision, but he didn't do that. He was decisive and let the chips fall where they may."[3]

Those close calls were the beginning of the end for Dickey, whose last two teams posted six and four wins, respectively. It was not a pretty parting. Someone spray-painted "Dump Dickey" on the field one night. Dickey saw the movement toward passing attacks in college football and was planning a transition in that direction, having hired former UF great Steve Spurrier as an offensive coach. He was relieved of his duties that same year, though, before the change ever took hold in Gainesville.

"If I had won a championship somewhere, [Florida] would have given me the time to make that transition," Dickey said. "You don't get that chance without a championship plaque on the wall."[4]

"I'll forever be thankful to Coach Doug Dickey," Spurrier said. "Not many coaches would hire a guy like me after 10 years in the NFL with my background and no

---

[3]Frenette, "As Gators-Volunteers Game Nears."

[4]Ibid.

coaching experience. That was the year I knew I wanted more of it, that I wanted to be a coach. Coach Dickey is one of my favorite people in the world. If I didn't get in then, maybe I don't get into it at all."[5]

Dickey was 58–43–2 at the Gators helm but just .500 in SEC games. He was 7–2 against Miami, including the seven-game streak. "We had better players than they did for that particular period of time," he said. "They went through several coaching changes in there and didn't quite get stabilized as well. . . . Miami was a well-respected program, and to this day is one of the outstanding programs in the country. We had great respect for Miami and the quality of the players that they brought to an intense rivalry."

Dickey eventually returned to Tennessee and continued his tremendous impact on the school and its athletics program. He replaced Woodruff for the second time in his career—this time as Volunteers AD. Under his leadership from 1985 to 2002, Tennessee won five SEC football championships and numerous national titles in other sports, while also upgrading its facilities across the board as one of the most respected programs in the conference. Dickey won the National Football Foundation's John Toner Award for his outstanding work as an administrator, and in 2003 was inducted into the College Football Hall of Fame.

---

[5]Pat Dooley, "Bittersweet Anniversary," *Gainesville Sun*, August 30, 1998.

The Dickey File

Name: Douglas Adair Dickey
Born: June 24, 1932, Vermillion, South Dakota
Playing career: University of Florida (1951–53)
Head coaching career: University of Tennessee (1964–69), University of Florida (1970–78)
Athletic director: University of Tennessee (1985–2002)

16

ORANGE CRUSHED TO THE POINT OF KICKING

GIVEN A CHANCE to revisit his controversial 1980 decision to kick a run-up-the-score field goal on the final play of a 31–7 romp over Florida, former Miami coach Howard Schnellenberger said he would handle it differently. But by no means was he apologizing.

"As years went by I kind of mellowed, and said I'd made a terrible mistake," Schnellenberger said. "I shouldn't have kicked the field goal. I should have sent the field goal team out and had the center snap it to the holder, and have him turn sideways towards the [Florida] student section, and we should have kicked it up into the student section. That would have been better."

Schnellenberger was livid because of a group of Florida fans—presumably students—in the east stands threw everything from ice to oranges to toilet paper rolls at the Miami sideline during the game. Despite his impressive victory, the Hurricanes coach did not flash a smile until about an hour after the game, when a reporter suggested that someday Miami might get an on-campus stadium and show some retribution.

"It was terrible. It was brutal. It was dangerous," Schnellenberger recalled in a recent interview. "Those bastards, the night before they get a whole crate of oranges—every fraternity got two or three crates of those damned oranges—and they plug them. And they force vodka down in there and then they put them in a deep freeze. They freeze them. They're the size of coconuts and as hard as bowling balls.

"And they take 'em up to the top of the stadium, seventy-six rows high, and they're lined up right behind the visiting team. . . . It was like incoming artillery. One hit my cheerleader and knocked her out. One hit my son, put him to the ground. And then the last one triggered my going out there and kicking a field goal."

The Hurricanes had recovered a late fumble, leading 28–7. Most coaches would have simply run out the clock. Not Schnellenberger. Not on this day. He called timeout with one second to play in order to get his field goal unit on the field.

The boot did more to set the tone for the UF-UM rivalry in the 1980s than anything that could have been said or done off the field, though there was plenty of that, too. Miami already loathed Florida as the school that kicked them around in the '70s, and the school that got all the in-state attention. The fact Schnellenberger ran up the score gave the Gators something to hate Miami for, too.

"We'll react to that 365 days from now," said Florida coach Charley Pell, meaning the following season.[1]

"Frank Broyles said on national television, that's unsportsmanlike and terrible," Schnellenberger said of the UF fans. "But I did that because I wanted somebody to know how dangerous it was out there, and after the game nobody tried to put a stop to it. So in the press conference, they asked me why I did it, and that's what I told them. I wanted people to know that was the worst hospitality ever shown."

The events of the day, and Schnellenberger's reaction, helped bring about change for the better. Florida students were subsequently moved to an end zone to keep them out of arm's reach of opposing teams. "I think we have great fans," Pell offered. "They're just so dadgummed hungry. They get frustrated, too. We just need to do a better job of helping them understand sportsmanship. We're certainly going to work at it."[2]

As fate would have it, the young man who made the late kick in that 1980 game also knocked home the winner the

---

[1]Ray Holliman, "Schnellenberger Does Job But Needs Support," *St. Petersburg Times*, December 1, 1980.

[2]Mike Cobb, "One Kick Revived Miami-Gator Rivalry," *Lakeland Ledger*, September 1, 1981.

following year in Miami, when tensions ran high but no large-scale retribution was enacted by fans. Danny Miller kicked a 55-yard field goal that banged off the left upright and tumbled over the crossbar with 45 seconds remaining to give the Hurricanes a 21–20 upset of the Gators at the Orange Bowl. It was the 1981 season opener, so there was no need to wait the 365 days Pell predicted. A partisan crowd of 73,817 in Miami went home jubilant.

Florida took a 14–3 lead at halftime before bowing to Miami's backup quarterback. Starter Jim Kelly, who scored the first Miami touchdown in the third quarter, was injured later in the period. Junior Mark Richt took over, hit Rocky Belk with a 55-yard touchdown pass to pull Miami within 20–18, and began the winning drive at the Miami 36-yard line with 2:48 to go.

"Late in the game I hit Glenn Dennison on a little crossing route, and got just enough range I think for Danny Miller to convince Coach [Schnellenberger] that he could kick it," Richt said. "I think Coach called timeout because Danny was kind of tugging on his jacket, saying he could make it. So he put the field goal team out there, and sure enough Danny made it."

It was the fourth consecutive win for Miami in the series that Florida had dominated for most of the 1970s. So when their September meeting in Gainesville came around in 1982, Gators fans were chomping—literally—to get after the Hurricanes. And given the projectiles that flew in the '80 game, measures were taken to ensure this one didn't get out of hand.

Campus police, the Gainesville PD, the Alachua County Sheriff's Office, and the Florida Highway Patrol all provided extra security measures for the game. Security was doubled on the east (Miami) side of the field, including placing guards right behind the bench.

The extra precautions paid off with a day free of major incidents, and the game featured a classic finish for the second year in a row. Miami appeared to be on the verge of dusting Florida for the fifth straight year when UF quarterback Wayne Peace connected with fullback James Jones on a spectacular 17-yard touchdown pass with 1:48 remaining. The one-handed grab at the goal line (Miami players contended Jones didn't actually cross the line) gave the Gators a 17–14 triumph over the fifteenth-ranked Hurricanes.

"I can't remember seeing a catch like that," Pell said. "That was a Willie Mays deluxe."[3]

Jones didn't remember seeing it, either. That's because he had been struggling with his contact lenses, so he removed them after the first few plays of the game. "It looked kind of fuzzy," he said, "so I just stuck my right hand up there and came down with it in the end zone."[4]

Florida students went berserk. And they kept any oranges to themselves.

---

[3]Ed Shearer, "Pell's Gators Overcome Miami," Associated Press story in the *Sumter Daily Item*, September 4, 1982.

[4]Ibid.

17

FLORIDA HANDS MIAMI ITS ONLY 1983 BLEMISH

MANY MONTHS AFTER Florida's convincing home win over Miami on September 3, 1983, bumper stickers began to emerge on the cars of Gator fans around the state. They read: "Florida 28, National Champs 3." That's because Miami rebounded from the early loss to win the rest of its games and claim the first national championship in the program's history. Their magical season began oh-so-humbly in Gainesville.

Charley Pell and Howard Schnellenberger had brought their Florida and Miami programs, respectively, to a place where they expected to compete with the best teams in the nation. The rivalry was running particularly hot thanks to some last-minute finishes, controversial decisions, and plenty of trash talk among players and fans in recent years. So it was not at all surprising that a record Florida Field gathering of 73,907 turned out to watch what was expected to be another close game.

It was no such thing, as the Gators raced out of the locker room and took immediate control. Florida took advantage of a Miami fumble deep in its own territory on the game's opening possession for a 7–0 lead two-and-a-half minutes into the game. Quarterback Wayne Peace completed his first eight passes, making it 14–0 on a nifty little toss to Joe Henderson on third-and-goal from the 2-yard line. Even trick plays worked for the Gators, including a 28-yard completion from the left-handed receiver Dwayne Dixon to Bee Lang that sparked a nine-play, 71-yard touchdown drive.

Peace was actually none too thrilled after the game, saying he felt his team could have scored at least two more touchdowns were it not for miscues. He also lamented the fact he finished the game completing just a total of 18 of 32 passes after the 8-for-8 start. "I wasn't as sharp tonight as last season, and we had more balls dropped tonight than we did maybe all of last year."[1]

Miami linebacker Ken Sisk, the game's top tackler, wasn't buying it. "We didn't execute the way we can, but he [Peace] did everything right tonight."[2]

---

[1]Michael Henry, "In the Locker Rooms," *St. Petersburg Evening Independent*, September 5, 1983.

[2]Ibid.

The Gators also dominated on defense and special teams. The defense made Miami quarterback Bernie Kosar's debut a rough one, forcing turnover after turnover. Punter David Nardone dropped three boots inside the Hurricanes' 10-yard line, pinning Kosar and Miami deep. "He was superhuman," Schnellenberger said.[3]

After the loss, Schnellenberger made an important decision that he believes led to great things for the Hurricanes. Typically, he would have come down hard on his men for a subpar performance. His players had come to expect it. But this time, knowing the caliber of team he had in the works, there were no loud diatribes in the locker room, no extra wind sprints on the practice field, and no pointed words in the press. Schnellenberger decided instead to proceed in a business-as-usual manner. And before long, business as usual turned into a dynasty in Coral Gables.

"When I took them in the locker room I said, 'Boys, if we play that good every game we play, we're going to be OK—if we take our turnovers out,'" Schnellenberger said. "So instead of taking them out at four in the morning like I did in other games that we'd gotten beat at Miami, we treated it like we won the game. And they responded so well."

What made it easier for Schnellenberger to abandon his typical post-loss routine were the positives he saw up and down his roster. The coach saw Kosar stand tall in the pocket

---

[3]Ibid.

against an inspired UF defense. He saw playmakers all over the field. He saw future superstars Alonzo Highsmith on offense and Jerome Brown on defense. He saw a team that had a chance to be great, and he nurtured it along the way to becoming exactly that.

The Hurricanes shut out Purdue and Notre Dame in back-to-back weeks. They used victories over the Fighting Irish, Louisville, and West Virginia to begin their ascent toward the top of the national rankings. They trailed 16–7 midway through the third quarter in a tough regular-season finale at Tallahassee, but Kosar led them back. Down 16–14 with just over two minutes to go, he took them from midfield into chip-shot field goal range for a 17–16 win that set up an Orange Bowl date with Nebraska for the national championship.

The Cornhuskers were favored, but the game was on Miami's home turf, and by this time the team that lost to Florida in the opener had become the team that would dominate college football through the remainder of the 1980s. The Hurricanes scored the game's first 17 points and held on for a 31–30 triumph when safety Kenny Calhoun knocked down Turner Gill's two-point conversion pass.

The Hurricanes were national champions. And Florida fans had bumper stickers to buy up.

It could have turned out differently. Back then, a loss to Florida could have sent any number of Miami players into despair. "You almost felt like the season was over when we lost to them," said former UM linebacker Jay Brophy of the general feeling surrounding a loss to the Gators. "And if you beat 'em, no matter what, at least we beat Florida."[4]

The Hurricanes allowed just 7.8 points per game until the Orange Bowl after giving up 28 to Florida in the opener.

"Coach Schnellenberger and the coaches realized we had so much talent on this team that they couldn't destroy us mentally or physically because of this loss," Highsmith said of the approach the coaches took following the opening loss in Gainesville. "Let's treat it like we won, let's see how that works out, and it worked out perfect."[5]

Miami's 1983 National Championship

RECORD: 11–1

Date	Location	Winner	Score
September 3	at Florida	Florida Field, Gainesville, FL	L 3–28
September 10	at Houston	Astrodome, Houston, TX	W 29–7
September 17	Purdue	Orange Bowl, Miami, FL	W 35–0
September 24	Notre Dame	Orange Bowl, Miami, FL	W 20–0
October 1	at Duke	Wallace Wade Stadium, Durham, NC	W 56–17

(continued on next page)

---

[4]Andrea Adelson, "Miami Dynasty Born out of '83 Defeat," ESPN.com, September 4, 2013.

[5]Ibid.

October 8	Louisville	Orange Bowl, Miami, FL	W 42–14
October 15	at Mississippi State	Scott Field, Starkville, MS	W 31–7
October 22	at Cincinnati	Riverfront Stadium, Cincinnati, OH	W 17–7
October 29	West Virginia	Orange Bowl, Miami, FL	W 20–3
November 5	East Carolina	Orange Bowl, Miami, FL	W 12–7
November 12	at Florida State	Doak Campbell Stadium, Tallahassee, FL	W 17–16
January 2, 1984	vs. Nebraska	Orange Bowl, Miami, FL	W 31–30

18

KOSAR, MIAMI TURN ON ESPN'S LIGHTS

A LANDMARK SUPREME COURT decision broke up the NCAA's monopoly on television rights and allowed a fledgling sports cable network called ESPN to broadcast live college football games for the first time in 1984. Some accounts list the September 1 game between Miami and Florida at Tampa Stadium as the network's first live game. It actually lost that honor to BYU and Pittsburgh by about four hours. It was, however, the first-ever live night game on the network that would grow to become a colossus in the world of sports. And it was a prime-time telecast indeed.

Jim Simpson and Paul Maguire called a classic at "The Big Sombrero," the nickname given to the Tampa venue that hosted the NFL's Buccaneers on Sundays. Miami, coming off a national championship in '83, had just opened the season with a 20–18 upset of top-ranked Auburn in the Kickoff

Classic to stretch its winning streak to 12 straight games. First-year coach Jimmy Johnson had inherited a Cadillac and was eager to see where its driver, sophomore quarterback Bernie Kosar, could steer it.

Florida, ranked seventeenth entering the game, was simply trying to make some on-field news for a change. Coach Charley Pell had announced six days earlier that, in the wake of a twenty-month NCAA investigation into rules violations, he would resign at the end of the year. His Gators had been the last team to defeat the Hurricanes, and they were eager to send their coach out with another such victory despite having lost projected starting quarterback Dale Dorminey to a knee injury just days before the game.

With the cameras rolling and much of America getting its first live glimpse at a heated state rivalry, the teams traded punches on the scoreboard. Florida's Lorenzo Hampton snapped a 3–3, second-quarter tie when he took a pitch 64 yards for a touchdown. Four short field goals by Miami freshman Greg Cox and a 21-yard run by Darryl Oliver gave the Hurricanes a 19–10 cushion, but Bobby Raymond got UF within six in the third quarter when he booted his second field goal of the game.

Fourth-quarter turnovers hurt the Gators. Miami safety Ken Calhoun forced and recovered a fumble by Florida receiver Gary Rolle at the UM 1-yard line with 11:50 remaining. Less than five minutes later, UF punter Rick Tuten dropped the ball before he could get his foot on it.

Florida's defense was up to the challenge in both cases, and with less than a minute to play it was a freshman walk-on who led the Gators to a touchdown that looked like it would hold up as the game winner.

Kerwin Bell, making his debut at quarterback in place of Dorminey, converted two fourth downs on the late drive—one on an 8-yard pass to Ray McDonald and another on a QB keeper to the Miami 5. He then lobbed a touchdown pass to Frankie Neal on the next play to give Florida a 20–19 edge with 41 seconds remaining.

While Gators fans across the country were celebrating, Kosar was readying his offense for one last drive toward a thirteenth consecutive victory. Three quick completions and a dive up the middle, and the Hurricanes were in field goal range. Kosar took them 72 yards in just 29 seconds, and every one of the 72,000-plus fans in attendance (the largest Tampa crowd since the Super Bowl in January of that year) expected Miami—at the 12-yard line—to down the ball in the middle of the hash marks for a winning field goal attempt. Kosar and his head coach, however, had other plans.

"I think Bernie's eyes convinced me," Johnson said after the game. "Bernie said, 'Coach, I know I can do it.'"[1] What the quarterback did was loft a 12-yard touchdown pass to Eddie Brown in the left rear corner of the end zone with

---

[1]Paul Helgren, "Kosar Is in the Eye of the Hurricanes," *The Michigan Daily*, September 8, 1984.

seven seconds left in the game to end Florida's upset bid. On the game's final play, Miami's Tolbert Bain returned an interception 59 yards for a meaningless touchdown that set the final score of the thriller at 32–20.

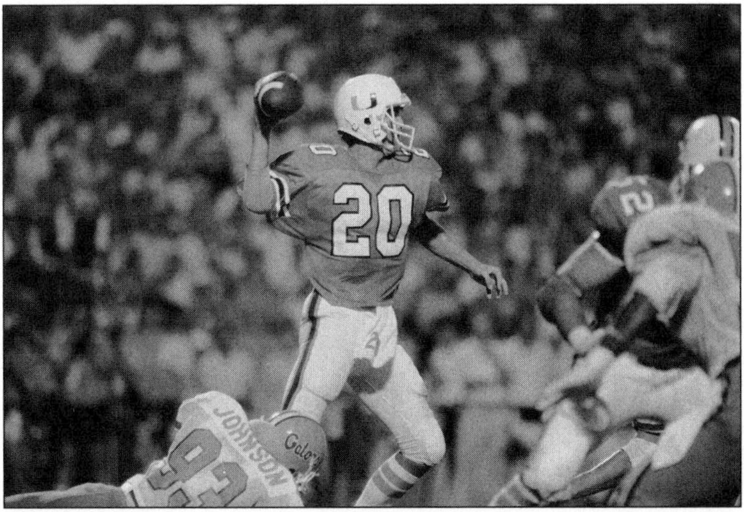

Sophomore quarterback Bernie Kosar tied a school record with 25 completions and passed for 300 yards as Miami surged past Florida, 32–20, in a 1984 game that was much closer than the final score might indicate. Kosar set single-season Hurricane records for passing yards and touchdowns that year. *AP Photo*

"They were in great field goal position and they throw a pass like that for a touchdown," Florida safety Roger Sibbald lamented. "No other team in America would have thrown the ball down there except Miami. They caught us off guard."[2]

[2]Associated Press, "Aerial Antics Win for Kosar, Flutie," *The Telegraph* (Nashua, NH), September 4, 1984.

Kosar tied a school record with 25 completions in 33 attempts and finished the game with 300 passing yards. That week, the Hurricanes vaulted all the way from No. 10 in the AP national rankings to No. 1. And a nationwide television audience witnessed the aggressive approach they would bring to the gridiron—and into living rooms around the country—for years to come.

"I think the next time on third and long in that situation," Johnson said, laughing, "teams will be playing pass defense."[3]

Astronomical Growth

Three decades after ESPN began airing live college football in 1984, the network's audience for the sport is nothing short of mind-boggling. A National Football Foundation report in 2015 found that, during the 2014 college football season:

- ESPN outlets reached more than 185.7 million viewers during regular-season telecasts.
- ESPN broadcasts of the college football playoff semifinals and national championship game combined to average 29.8 million viewers.
- Digitally, the 517 FBS games on Watch ESPN generated 1.2 billion live minutes viewed, an 80 percent increase over the previous year.

[3]Helgren, "Kosar Is in the Eye."

19

SCHNELLENBERGER: TRULY ONE OF A KIND

A RARE FEW MEN can be called "father" of a football program. A rarer few have fathered two of them. The single name on the latter list is a long one. It's Howard Schnellenberger.

When Miami and Florida Atlantic lined up to open the 2013 season in Miami, each school welcomed an honorary captain—the man called "father" of each program—to the game. Miami turned to Schnellenberger. So did Florida Atlantic.

"That was the genesis of the game, that we would celebrate what he has done for both programs, really starting both programs at the end of the day," said then-Miami coach Al Golden. "He's a man who owes me nothing but treats me with great respect and imparts great wisdom every time

I see him. We're blessed to have him in our family. I know FAU probably feels the same way."[1]

The game was played thirty years after Schnellenberger brought Miami's program from good to elite with a 1983 national championship that set the Hurricanes on a path to dominance. He set the foundation by which "The U" came to be judged.

Schnellenberger started the Florida Atlantic program from scratch in 1998, building toward a 2001 debut in which the Owls won four of 10 games. Two years later, he coached them to an 11–3 mark. He said of FAU before that 2013 contest in Miami, "This is my team."[2]

There were no doubts about Schnellenberger's loyalties in the 1980s. They were squarely with Miami—the city and the school. The Indiana native and lifelong football man was in his second tour as offensive coordinator with the NFL's Miami Dolphins, whom he helped to an undefeated season in '72, when the Hurricanes came calling in '79. He was the only coach they seriously considered for the job.

"I obviously wouldn't have made the change from professional to college, especially with the Dolphins back in the playoff picture now, unless I was planning on committing

---

[1]ESPN.com wire services, "Teams Laud Howard Schnellenberger," ESPN.com, August 27, 2013.

[2]Ibid.

a lot of time here," said Schnellenberger, who spent two years as head coach of the Baltimore Colts.

"I feel the program is healthy. The commitment is here for football. Lou Saban has done a good job here, but it wasn't to the point that the job is done."[3]

The colorful Schnellenberger arrived as a reporter's dream, if not a player's right from the start. He spoke his mind and ruffled a few feathers. A disciple of Alabama coach Bear Bryant, he put his players through rigorous conditioning designed to give them an edge in battle. He also recognized the deep pool of talent in the Miami area and vowed to keep those athletes from leaving for Florida or Florida State.

Mostly, Schnellenberger breathed fire into a program that stood on shaky ground when he took over. A smaller private school, Miami had considered dropping the football program due to financial struggles. Instead, Schnellenberger inspired the school to reach for new heights, insisting that success breeds profitability.

"My junior year, we voted 6–5 to keep football," said Art Kehoe, who went on to become an assistant coach under Schnellenberger. "We were going to drop football, and he took it from there to a national title. The guy's an unbelievable coach. . . . Heck, we couldn't pay the phone bill.

---

[3]Associated Press, "Miami Hires Schnellenberger," *Daytona Beach Journal*, January 9, 1979.

And now we've got five national titles and played for 11 of them, and he's the main fabric of all that. He started it all."[4]

The Hurricanes had not won more than six games in a season since 1967. Schnellenberger needed just one year of building to get them pointed in the right direction. After going 5–6 in his first season, his '80 and '81 teams won nine games apiece, the former capping the year with a victory in the Peach Bowl. It was Miami's first bowl appearance in thirteen years and first bowl victory since '66.

With a strong nucleus of talent stockpiled from Florida, like soon-to-be All-America receiver Eddie Brown and top rusher Albert Bentley, Schnellenberger began boosting the lineup with national-caliber recruits, too. It was not a hard sell luring top Midwestern prep stars with an up-and-coming program, a pro-style offense that was starting to change college football, and the beauty of South Beach. Bernie Kosar brought his 6'5" frame and accurate arm from Youngstown, Ohio, while fellow Ohioan Jay Brophy (Akron) arrived to anchor the defense. Standout tight end Glenn Dennison was the pride of Beaver Falls, Pennsylvania. Schnellenberger had a national contender in the making.

It all came together in 1983. After an opening loss to Florida—Schnellenberger's second loss in five games against the Gators—Miami ran the table and captured the first national championship in school history. The Canes toppled

---

[4]ESPN.com wire services, "Teams Laud Schnellenberger.

Notre Dame, West Virginia, and Florida State, the latter 17–16 on a last-second field goal. The icing was a 31–30 thriller over No. 1-ranked Nebraska in the Orange Bowl. "Miracle in Miami" screamed the *Sports Illustrated* cover.

"After we got by the loss against Florida and the first half against Houston, we had pretty much smooth sailing [until late in the season]," Schnellenberger said. "We were never ahead against Florida and we lost badly. But almost to a man, our football team graded out as winners. We did have a better team than we thought we had coming out of that loss."[5]

Howard Schnellenberger brought Miami football to prominence between 1979 and '83. Finding a way to keep the huge South Florida talent pool to stay home, he coached the Hurricanes to their first national championship in his final season at the helm. *AP Photo/Doug Jennings*

[5]Associated Press, "Miami Wins National Title," *Ocala Star-Banner*, January 4, 1984.

After the national title, something perhaps even more shocking took place. Schnellenberger gave up his post to become head coach of the Washington Federals of the fledgling United States Football League, a professional rival to the NFL. The Federals were planning to move from Washington to Miami, which appealed to the man who had spent twelve years of his coaching career in South Florida.

In August 1984, however, the relocation fell through. So as his Hurricanes were preparing to defend their championship under first-year coach Jimmy Johnson, Schnellenberger began job hunting. "I'm a football coach by trade and I plan to be one for a long time to come," he said. "I'm sorry that it's not going to be in Miami, though."[6]

Schnellenberger landed on his feet, of course. In addition to starting the FAU program and coaching briefly in what he considers a failed year at Oklahoma, he spent 10 years at the Louisville helm turning around his hometown school between 1985 and '94. He led the school to its fourth- and fifth-ever bowl appearances. He won both, including a win over Alabama in the 1991 Fiesta Bowl.

Still a huge fan of college football and its traditions, it pained Schnellenberger to see the Florida-Miami rivalry disappear from the schools' annual schedule in the late 1980s.

---

[6]Associated Press, "Schnellenberger Is Left Without Coaching Job," *Toledo Blade*, August 25, 1984.

Not surprisingly, he takes a pro-Hurricane stance when it comes to his hope for its renewal.

"Every one of the games was the biggest game on our schedule," he said. "Every one of those games was a time when the whole campus came alive. The old-timers, Walter Kichefski and all those guys who played back in the '50s and the '40s, came out of the woodwork. Some of them came out of the bars. Some of them came out of the lawyer's office or corporations. They came with their emotional stockpile on the line, and it took on a life-and-death kind of a situation. The student body picked up on that. The players picked up on it from the students and the alumni.

"They don't have to play one of those 'gimmes,'" Schnellenberger said of the Gators scheduling one "easy" opponent to go along with their SEC schedule and annual date with Florida State. "But they think [adding a game against Miami] makes the schedule too tough, I guess. . . . It's going to take an act of God and the hard work of Floridians. It may have to come from the legislature. But something has to be done."

The Schnellenberger File

Name: Howard Leslie Schnellenberger
Born: March 16, 1934, Saint Meinrad, Indiana
Playing career: University of Kentucky (1952–56)
Head coaching career: Baltimore Colts (1973–74), University of Miami (1979–83), University of Louisville (1985–94), Oklahoma University (1995), Florida Atlantic University (2001–11)

20

FOR BETTER OR WORSE, PELL LEFT MARK AT UF

THE MENTION OF Charley Pell conjures emotions of one form or another for those who follow Florida football. The good: an amazing turnaround from 0–10–1 in 1979 to 8–4 in 1980; the Gators' first AP Top Ten finish (1983); several improvements to Florida Field, including the addition of luxury suites; and a passion for winning that few could match. And the ugly: charges for 107 NCAA violations; sanctions levied for 59 of those offenses; and Pell's firing three games into the '84 season.

Oh, and he won just two of six games against Miami.

"Did I violate some rules? Yes," Pell once told the NBC news program *Dateline*. "Does that make me a cheater? If it does, yes I am. There wasn't room for anything but winning. Nothing. Winning was the sole obsession, to a fault."[1]

Pell's fixation with winning was a plus with Florida administrators when they plucked him from Clemson in 1979. The Gators had struggled to a 10–11–1 record in their last two seasons under Doug Dickey, while Pell was revitalizing Clemson over that same span. In his only two years at the Tigers' helm, he led them to the Gator Bowl in '77 and to an ACC championship in '78. He earned ACC Coach of the Year honors after each of those seasons.

It did not surface until after his hiring at Florida that Pell had committed NCAA recruiting violations at Clemson, which ultimately landed the program two years' probation. From Florida's vantage point, Pell was the perfect man for the job. He had won a national championship and earned All-SEC honors as an undersized lineman under Alabama coach Bear Bryant in his home state. He coached for Bryant as a graduate assistant, a great springboard into his own head coaching career.

Pell hated losing, and in his 1979 debut the Gators did not win a game. As much as it pained him, he kept his eye on upgrading the talent level and recruited talent galore. Progress came quickly. The one-year jump to 8–4 in 1980 was unprecedented in school history. It was the first of four

---

[1]Frank Litsky, "Charley Pell Is Dead at 60; Ousted as Florida Coach," *New York Times*, May 30, 2001.

straight years in which his Gators posted a winning record and earned a bowl game invitation. They went 9–2–1 in '83, defeating Iowa in the Gator Bowl.

By then, however, the NCAA was onto Pell. He announced before the '84 slate that he planned to retire at season's end. When the NCAA announced three games into the year that it was looking into 107 charges of wrongdoing, UF did not give him that luxury. Pell was sent packing, and offensive coordinator Galen Hall elevated to interim coach. Hall took the Gators to their first SEC championship that fall, though it turned out to be short-lived.

In '85, the NCAA levied sanctions for 59 various rules violations under Pell, including making cash payments and loans to athletes, allowing walk-ons to stay in athletic dorms, and spying on at least seven opponents' practices. Florida was placed on three years' probation (later reduced to two), stripped of scholarships, and banned from bowl games and television appearances for two years. The Gators were also forced to vacate their only SEC football championship.

Pell accepted the blame, a decision he later said he might have taken to the extreme. "I took the blame for everything to exonerate every other coach on the staff," he offered. "I always believed I did too good a job of that. All it did was cause a lot of grief. I made mistakes. They were my mistakes; I was the leader. I trusted some people I shouldn't have. The mistakes and errors I made did not make the difference in the football program. Those mistakes and errors disgust and embarrass me."[2]

Some UF boosters felt Pell got a raw deal. At a time when cheating was fairly rampant in Division I sports—and before the advent of twenty-four-hour sports news that helped expose it—some felt Pell was turned into a scapegoat. One famous Gator booster in that category was New York Yankees owner George Steinbrenner, never one to shy away from controversy.

"It's a crime in many ways," Steinbrenner claimed in 1984. "The system has been created and the coaches aren't at fault. I coached at Northwestern and Purdue, I was on the board of regents for the state of Ohio and I'm a team owner, so I can speak from having seen all sides. I've been in locker rooms probably longer than Charley Pell. . . .What happens is that the alumni scream for a winner and the administration wants a program that's within the rules. The poor coach is caught in the middle. It would be fine if everyone agreed to follow the rules, but 99 percent break them. I don't care what the school is, [the NCAA] should check into all teams that play in bowls."[3]

While the punishment for the Gators was painful, the toll it took on Pell was far greater. He never earned another

---

[2]Ibid.

[3]Jim Martz, "Pell Made a Scapegoat: Steinbrenner," Knight News Service in the *Lakeland Ledger*, September 4, 1984.

college coaching job, though he longed to coach. He was treated for clinical depression. He attempted suicide ten years after his dismissal from UF. He became an advocate for suicide prevention and treatment for depression and other mental illnesses.

"I avoided it all my life," he said. "If I hadn't failed in an attempt on my life, I would have died not knowing what was wrong with me or that I had a problem. . . . The message is so critical to get out. I learned the hard way that there is an illness called depression, and I put that in capital letters. It's an ILLNESS. It's no different than high blood pressure; it's no different than diabetes. It has a cause, it has an effect, it has symptoms, it has medication, and it's manageable."[4]

Pell enjoyed a successful career in real estate before his death from lung cancer, at age sixty, in 2001.

The Pell File

Name: Charles Byron Pell
Born: February 17, 1941, Albertville, Alabama
Died: May 29, 2001, Gadsden, Alabama
Playing career: University of Alabama (1961–63)
Head coaching career: Jacksonville State (1969–73), Clemson University (1977–78), University of Florida (1979–84)

[4]Terry Dean, "Former Coach Sheds Light on Problems of Depression," *Cherokee County Herald*, September 16, 1998.

21

A LANDMARK DAY AT ORANGE BOWL

SEPTEMBER 7, 1985, is not exactly a date that gives Florida or Miami fans pause. Perhaps it should, though. Before a record crowd of 80,277 at the Orange Bowl, Kerwin Bell threw four touchdown passes to lead Florida to a 35–23, season-opening triumph over Miami. It avenged the Gators' only loss of the previous season. At the time of the game, that seemed like the most compelling story line. However, events of the next nine years gave that 1985 contest greater historical significance.

The next time Miami lost a home game was September 24, 1994. Its 58-game home winning streak remains an NCAA record as of this writing.

At the time of their win, it was the Gators who were surging. They came to Miami ranked fifth in the nation, and the victory was their tenth in a row. Bell had taken college football by storm as a freshman the prior fall, directing the Gators to a Southeastern Conference title and winning the SEC Player of the Year Award. He picked up where he left off against Miami, completing 20 of 28 passes for 248 yards and all four UF touchdowns—two to receiver Ricky Nattiel.

For a while, it looked like it was going to be a reasonably easy win. The Gators drove 80 yards on 14 plays following the opening kickoff for the first Bell-to-Nattiel touchdown. Miami tied the score early in the second quarter, but a Hurricane turnover and a surprise UF onside kick helped the Gators score ten points in the final six seconds of the half for a 20–7 lead at the break.

Vinny Testaverde, quarterbacking his first game for Miami, got the record crowd on its feet while leading a second-half comeback. The Canes dominated the third quarter, and Testaverde scored on a 13-yard scramble two plays into the fourth to give his team its only lead of the game, 21–20. The UM defense had been all over Bell in the Florida backfield, and the quarterback had a message for his linemen on the sideline.

"Last year I got time to throw the pass and then watch the receiver catch it and run with it," Bell told his teammates after Miami grabbed the lead. "The rest of tonight, all I ask is enough time to throw the pass. They can bury me, and I won't see the catch, but I'll get the ball to 'em if y'all will just give me time to throw it."[1]

---

[1]Jack Hairston, "Kerwin Bell's Legend Grows," *Gainesville Sun*, September 9, 1985.

A modest request, by all accounts, and the Gators obliged. Bell took some big hits in the fourth quarter, but threw two more touchdown passes to lift his team to victory. He gave Florida the lead for good on a 16-yard strike to Nattiel with 7:50 left in the game, and added an 8-yarder to Frankie Neal with 2:45 on the clock.

Miami defensive tackle Jerome Brown stops Florida's Neal Anderson from crossing the goal line during the second quarter of a 1985 game in Miami. Anderson and the Gators got the last word despite the goal-line stand, though, handing the Hurricanes a 35–23 setback. *AP Photo/Chris O'Meara*

Perhaps UF coach Galen Hall would have been more positive about the win had he known about the Orange Bowl winning streak the Hurricanes were about to launch. As it was, Hall was concerned about penalties, inconsistency, and sloppy play on special teams. Four Gator kickoffs went out of bounds, and twice UF was penalized for having too many men on the field for punt returns.

"We've got to become a complete football team," he said. "We can't have these ups and downs (and still) be rated that high."[2]

Testaverde, who had spent the previous two seasons backing up Bernie Kosar, had made a bold prediction three days before the game. He said Miami would roll to a 24–0 win. Despite the loss (and perhaps the lesson that such talk might be better saved for *after* games), he made a solid debut as the starter. He completed 24 of 40 passes for 278 yards, though he did fire two interceptions.

"When I stood on the sideline, I tried not to be just a spectator," Testaverde said of his time backing up Kosar. "I wanted to get something out of the game. See what the defense was doing, see what Bernie was doing. I was just trying to learn as much as I could. The competition made both of us better."[3]

The Gators went on to finish 9–1–1 in 1985, attaining the top national ranking in the Associated Press poll at one point, but were not eligible to play in a bowl game because of NCAA sanctions levied earlier in the year.

---

[2]Ken Hornack, "Gator Win Was Not Without Its Flaws," *Daytona Beach Sunday News-Journal*, September 9, 1985.

[3]Curt Holbreich, "Patience Pays Off," *Pittsburgh Press*, December 29, 1985.

Testaverde and the Hurricanes recovered splendidly from the loss, running the table on the rest of their regular-season opponents. Eight of those 10 wins came by double-digit margins, the only exceptions being a 35–27 win at Florida State and a 29–22 win at Maryland on back-to-back weeks. They were ranked second in the nation before falling to eighth-ranked Tennessee in the Sugar Bowl.

And, somewhere out west, the players who would grow up to become the next group of visitors to beat Miami at the Orange Bowl had not even entered high school yet, probably having no idea they would attend the University of Washington.

22

MIAMI TOPPLES FLORIDA EN ROUTE TO 1987 CHAMPIONSHIP

HURRICANES COACH JIMMY Johnson once said he didn't see the Florida-Miami rivalry as a bitter one. At least one of his players vehemently disagreed. Junior linebacker George Mira Jr., in 1986, said he didn't like anything about Florida—the school or the football team.

"Ever since I was a kid, it was 'Hate the Gators, hate the Gators, hate the Gators,'" said Mira, the son of Miami All-America quarterback George Mira Sr. "There's a little something extra you'll put into every play because of that. Even if you're tired, you'll try a little harder. . . .They're all Gators. They're the kind of school where everybody thinks any other school is nothing."[1]

---

[1]Wire reports, "Mira Sees Special UM-Gator Rivalry," *Boca Raton News*, September 4, 1986.

One thing is certain—no analyst in college football thought for one second that the Hurricanes were nothing. Most saw them as one of a small handful of national title contenders when the 1986 slate kicked off. After a 34–14 romp at South Carolina to open the year, the superlatives were flying.

"My God," said South Carolina coach Joe Morrison. "They are like a pro team."[2]

Ironically, it had been the *loser* of the Florida-Miami game that had challenged for the national title the previous three years by going undefeated in the remainder of their regular-season games. Miami did so in 1983, going 11–1; Florida rallied in '84, overcoming its loss to UM with a 9–1–1 season; and the Hurricanes ripped off 10 straight wins following their opening loss to UF in '85.

Johnson was willing to take his chances that a win at Gainesville in '86 might be better than a loss in trying to guide the Canes to their second national championship, and he had to admit the rivalry with the Gators was reaching new heights given the caliber of football both teams were playing.

"It's turned into a great rivalry," said Florida quarterback Kerwin Bell, "because both teams have been ranked high in the polls the last few years. Any time you have two great teams like that within the state, it naturally causes a rivalry."[3]

---

[2]Jim Achenbach, "Storm Warning: Hurricanes Put Gators on Alert," *Sarasota Herald-Tribune*, September 1, 1986.

[3]Associated Press, "Hurricanes, Gators to Air Out Rivalry," *Boca Raton News,* September 6, 1986.

Bell entered the 1986 game against the Hurricanes with a 19–2–2 record. However, it was Miami's Vinny Testaverde who would go on to win the Heisman Trophy that year. And it was Testaverde whose team flexed its muscle September 6 in Gainesville, ending UF's 21-game home unbeaten string.

Melvin Bratton ran for 20- and 24-yard touchdowns and Testaverde threw a TD pass to Michael Irvin as the Hurricanes rolled to a 23–15 victory. The UM defense was relentless, sacking Bell six times and recovering four Florida fumbles.

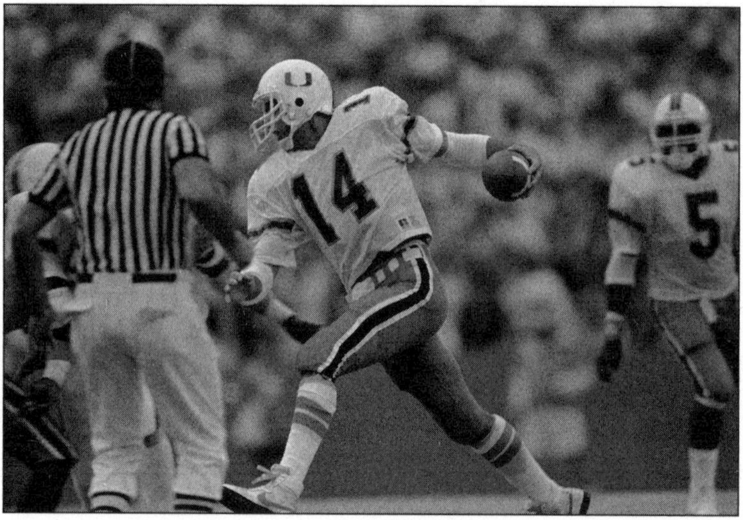

On his way to the 1986 Heisman Trophy, quarterback Vinny Testaverde and the Hurricanes ended a 21-game home win streak by Florida with a 23–15 victory. Testaverde connected with fellow future NFL star Michael Irvin in the win. *AP Photo*

It was the second straight impressive victory for the Canes, and there were more to come. Miami knocked off top-ranked Oklahoma, 28–16, later the same month to grab the No.

1 ranking and whipped the remainder of its regular-season opponents by two touchdowns or more. The Hurricanes' national championship dreams ended in a memorable Fiesta Bowl, however, when Penn State silenced their swagger in a 14–10 upset.

By the time Florida visited the Orange Bowl to open the 1987 season, everyone knew it might be the last time in a long while the two rivals would meet. The Gators had decided to discontinue the series due to their SEC commitments and an annual game against Florida State, a fellow state school.

It was not a popular decision among the Miami faithful, but the Canes players decided to concentrate on the factors they could control. They dressed a tackling dummy in a No. 12 Gator jersey and spent the week leading up to the game hitting the Bell "likeness."

They continued the onslaught against the real Bell on game day. They sacked him five times, picked off three of his passes and held him to a 15-for-32 completion rate before knocking him out of the game with a shoulder injury in the fourth quarter. Florida coughed up six turnovers in the game.

"My worst fears came true," Florida coach Galen Hall lamented. "We were a young team offensively and went up against maybe the best defense in the country. Between their skills and our mistakes, we were overwhelmed."[4]

---

[4]United Press International, "Miami Proves It's Nobody's Dummy, Rips Florida, 31–4," *Pittsburgh Press*, September 6, 1987.

Sophomore Steve Walsh, replacing Testaverde at quarterback for the Hurricanes, enjoyed a great debut. He completed 17 of 24 passes for 234 yards and a touchdown to Brian Blades in a 31–4 blowout. "I knew our defense would do a good job," Walsh said after the win. "But I didn't know they would do that great a job."[5]

"I'm extremely proud of Walsh, his composure and his poise," said Johnson, whose Hurricanes got three field goals from Greg Cox, a 14-yard touchdown dash from Cleveland Gary, and a 41-yard interception return for a touchdown from Randy Shannon. "This is a happy day, but then again it is also a sad day because it's the last game of the series for a while. We were fortunate to win three of the last four games."[6]

Johnson's Hurricanes did not reminisce for long about their recent run of success against the Gators. Loaded with the kind of talent that made them the envy of college football and bravado to match their skill, Miami was on a mission.

They followed the win over Florida with back-to-back road victories over Top 10 schools Arkansas and Florida State, squeaking past the Seminoles 26–25. They hammered the schools in the middle of their schedule before finishing the regular season with another set of back-to-back wins against

---

[5]Associated Press, "Hurricanes Find Another QB," *Milwaukee Journal*, September 6, 1987.

[6]Ibid.

Top 10 opponents: Notre Dame and South Carolina—both at the Orange Bowl.

Finally, Miami returned to the top of college football for the second time in five years. As it happened, the national championship was decided on their home field, where the Hurricanes were in the middle of a 58-game winning streak. Even powerful Oklahoma, ranked No. 1, was unable to stop the game's brash, bold, immovable force. Second-ranked Miami won, 20–14, finishing a perfect 12–0 season.

"When the game ended, I gave a big sigh of relief," Johnson said. "We've been under the gun for a while around here. Winning the national championship is even more satisfying than it would normally be because we've come so close the last couple of years."[7]

Miami's 1987 National Championship

RECORD: 12–0

September 5	Florida	Orange Bowl, Miami, FL	W 31–4
September 26	at Arkansas	War Memorial Stadium, Little Rock, AR	W 51–7
October 3	at Florida State	Doak Campbell Stadium, Tallahassee, FL	W 26–25

(continued on next page)

[7]Bruce Lowitt, "Miami Memories," *St. Petersburg Times*, December 28, 2001.

October 10	Maryland	Orange Bowl, Miami, FL	W 46–16
October 24	at Cincinnati	Riverfront Stadium, Cincinnati, OH	W 48–10
October 31	at East Carolina	Ficklen Memorial Stadium, Greenville, NC	W 41–3
November 7	Miami (OH)	Orange Bowl, Miami, FL	W 54–3
November 14	Virginia Tech	Orange Bowl, Miami, FL	W 27–13
November 21	Toledo	Orange Bowl, Miami, FL	W 24–14
November 28	Notre Dame	Orange Bowl, Miami, FL	W 24–0
December 5	South Carolina	Orange Bowl, Miami, FL	W 20–16
January 1, 1988	vs. Oklahoma	Orange Bowl, Miami, FL	W 20–14

23

JOHNSON DOMINATES THE ODDS

THE CONSENSUS WAS clear upon Jimmy Johnson's hiring as University of Miami head football coach in 1984. Everyone agreed his task would be a tall one. He was replacing Howard Schnellenberger, "father" of the Hurricanes program in many ways, and the man who had guided the team to a national title the previous season. In addition to having to fill sizeable shoes at a program that now had sizeable expectations, the timing of Johnson's hire could hardly have been worse.

Schnellenberger, after landing a top recruiting class, resigned to become president, general manager, and head coach of a USFL professional team that was supposed to move from Washington, DC, to Miami for the '84 season. That move never happened, leaving Schnellenberger suddenly hunting for a job. The Hurricanes also hired Johnson, who had compiled a 29–25–3 record in five years at Oklahoma State, in June—*after* spring practice. And they gave him a schedule that, in 1984, included eight schools that made bowl games the previous year. Auburn and Michigan were among them.

"If I could have changed anything, it was the time I was hired," said Johnson, a Texan who was a defensive lineman under Frank Broyles at Arkansas and served as an assistant under the likes of Broyles, Johnny Majors (Iowa State), Jackie Sherrill (Pittsburgh), and Chuck Fairbanks (Oklahoma). "I wish I could have been here for spring practice. The schedule was in place when I got here, so there was nothing I could do about it."[1]

That, however, should be the end of any sympathy for Johnson. Though he took over a program that had just reached the pinnacle of college football, it was also one that was poised for future greatness. It had Bernie Kosar, a Heisman Trophy candidate, as its starting quarterback and an athletic defense that was beginning to dominate like none other.

If some Miami fans didn't know much about Johnson at first, they learned quickly after he beat Auburn and Florida in a six-day stretch to begin his career at the Hurricanes' helm. The Associated Press vaulted Miami to No. 1 in the country after those two games.

---

[1]Michael Janofsky, "Miami's New Coach Faces a Difficult Task This Season," *New York Times* News Service in the *Gainesville Sun,* August 27, 1984.

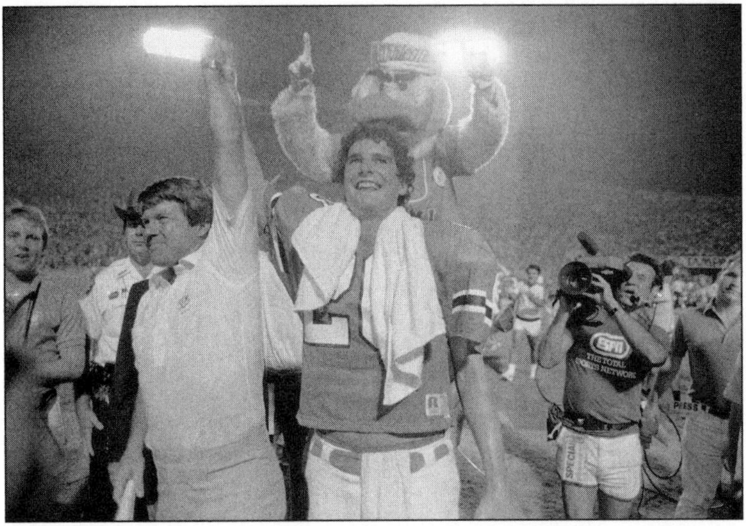

Miami coach Jimmy Johnson (left) and quarterback Bernie Kosar seemed on top of the world after coming from behind to knock off Florida, 32–20, in a 1984 game in Tampa. Three years later, Johnson and the Canes were truly on top of the college football world when they celebrated a national title. *AP Photo/Joe Skipper*

That ended with a loss to Michigan the following week, and the Canes went on to finish 8–5. They dropped their last three games by two points apiece—one after leading Maryland 31–0 at halftime, one on the most famous Hail Mary finish in college football history (Boston College's Doug Flutie), and a final heartbreaker to UCLA in the Fiesta Bowl.

Being a few points away from greatness would not suffice with Johnson or his players. Not only did he turn them loose to be brash and bold in their dominance, he set the tone himself. He was not afraid to score "insurance" touchdowns in the fourth quarter or to say when he thought his team was better, which was almost always. When it came to "bigger, stronger, faster," Johnson preached—and steadfastly recruited—the latter.

"Speed is the single most important ingredient for a football team," Johnson said. "A lot of my kids come from inner-city backgrounds. I think that's one of the reasons Miami doesn't get a lot of respect, because your average football fan might not relate to that."[2]

Johnson's Hurricanes talked, taunted, and danced their way past the best in college football for the next three years. The 1986 team, kept from a national title by an upset Fiesta Bowl loss to Penn State, might have been their best. Thirty-four players from their Fiesta Bowl roster that year were drafted by NFL teams. Of those, 28 played in the league.

Among the best were quarterback Vinny Testaverde, the 1986 Heisman Trophy winner; backup quarterback Steve Walsh; safety Bennie Blades; defensive lineman Jerome Brown; running back Alonzo Highsmith; and wide receiver Michael Irvin, who went on to win three Super Bowl championships with the Dallas Cowboys—two under Johnson's tutelage.

"In 1986 I had the best football team I've ever seen and we didn't win the national championship," Johnson said. "That will haunt me."[3]

---

[2]Greg Garber, "No Matching the Talent of 1986 Miami Hurricanes," *Hartford Courant*, December 22, 1992.

[3]Armando Salguero, "Johnson No Longer Haunted by Consecutive Bowl Losses," Cox News Service, *Spartanburg Herald-Journal*, January 2, 1989.

Walsh took over as starting quarterback in 1987, leading the Hurricanes to a perfect 12–0 record and their second national championship in school history. A 26–25 thriller at Florida State in the third game of the year and a 20–16 win over South Carolina in the regular-season finale were the only close calls as the Canes ran the table. Top-ranked Oklahoma was favored in the Orange Bowl, but there was no beating Miami in its hometown. The Hurricanes shut down the Sooner wishbone and took a 20–14 victory for the crown.

"This means the world to Coach Johnson," Irvin said after the game. "It gets the monkey off his back and everything. He won the biggest game in college football today. What can they say about him now? He's our coach, we're going to talk about him. But if anyone else is going to talk about him, that's when we get the attitude."[4]

"We had to play against a great style of offense tonight," Oklahoma coach Barry Switzer said. "I'm glad for Jimmy Johnson."[5]

Florida State entered the following season with the No. 1 ranking in the land, but a 31–0 drubbing at the hands of the Hurricanes made Miami the top-ranked team again. The Hurricanes' only loss in 1988 was a controversial 31–30 decision at Notre Dame, which went on to win the national title.

---

[4]United Press International, "Miami Beats Sooners to Claim National Title," *Ellensburg Daily Record*, January 2, 1988.

[5]Ibid.

A fight in the tunnel before that game was started by the Fighting Irish, by all accounts, but by then the Hurricanes' reputation preceded them. They were going to be blamed, regardless.

"It was good vs. evil, and we were evil," said former Miami sports information director Rich Dalrymple. "Maybe that scared people a little."[6]

Though he won just won national crown, Johnson averaged an 11–1 record over his final four seasons at Miami. His five-year record with the Hurricanes was 52–9.

Johnson took over the Dallas Cowboys in 1989 and, showing a keen preference to drafting Miami players, won back-to-back Super Bowls after the '92 and '93 seasons. He opened a Miami restaurant called Three Rings, commemorating his three football championships, and has gone on to great success as an NFL analyst on FOX television.

The Johnson File

Name: James William Johnson
Born: July 16, 1943, Port Arthur, Texas
Playing career: University of Arkansas
Head coaching career: Oklahoma State University (1979–83), University of Miami (1984–88), Dallas Cowboys (1989–93), Miami Dolphins (1996–99)

---

[6]Garber, "No Matching the Talent."

24

NO HALL PASS FOR GALEN

THE GALEN HALL era at the University of Florida was a roller coaster that included overcoming NCAA sanctions, getting into further NCAA trouble, winning an SEC championship, having that crown stripped, claiming a national Coach of the Year accolade and, finally, getting fired. Quite a résumé for a period of a little more than five years, after which Gator fans were thrilled to welcome Steve Spurrier to the post.

It could hardly have started any better for Hall, despite the powder keg he inherited when Florida fired Charley Pell three games into the 1984 slate due to NCAA sanctions under his watch. Hall, a former star quarterback at Penn State who played briefly in the NFL (Washington Redskins) and AFL (New York Jets), was elevated from offensive coordinator to interim head coach after a 1–1–1 start and promptly guided the Gators to eight consecutive wins and the SEC title. The Associated Press named him Coach of the Year, and some media outlets and computers even called the Gators national champs, though BYU topped the final polls.

The following May, UF didn't have either a national title or a conference crown to show for 1984. SEC coaches voted to strip Florida of the league title in the wake of the NCAA violations under Pell. Hall also had to deal with debilitating scholarship limitations, a lack of television exposure, and a ban from bowl games as part of the mess he took over, yet he managed to keep the Gators competitive.

Florida duplicated its 9–1–1 record in 1985, with Kerwin Bell again directing a potent attack. The Gators actually attained a No. 1 AP national ranking that year following a 14–10 November victory at Auburn, but a loss to Georgia the following week cost them a shot at national title consideration.

Scholarship limits began taking their toll in '86, when UF slipped to 6–5. Hall certainly felt the frustrations of Gator boosters and alumni, but was known as a man who could keep football in perspective.

"Football is very important to those who are playing the game," he said that September, "but it is not the ultimate thing in your life. You need to keep in perspective the fact this is not a life-or-death matter or World War III. There must be self-sacrifice and discipline in order to achieve athletic success, but there must also be fun playing the sport."[1]

Florida fans had fun watching Emmitt Smith run the football in '87. Though the sanctions still stung, the Gators returned to bowl play. They fell 20–16 to UCLA in the Aloha Bowl and finished 6–6. The '88 squad improved to 7–5 despite losing five of its last six regular-season games, and edged Illinois 14–10 in the All-American Bowl.

With one of the best ground attacks in the country and improving talent across the board, the Gators appeared to be on the cusp of regaining national prominence—something their rivals from Miami had come to dominate in recent years.

It would happen without Hall, however. The coach had been on the proverbial hot seat entering the '89 season while fans continued to wait for the breakthrough. An impressive 4–1 start, including a 16–13 victory at LSU on October 7, had some of the naysayers beginning to believe.

It was what the NCAA believed, though, that mattered most. Or, rather, what college sports' governing body knew. Hall had been paying some of his assistant coaches out of his own pocket, violating NCAA caps on their salaries. There were also allegations that he had paid the legal expenses of a player, though Hall denied the latter charge.

---

[1]Billy Mitchell, "Rally Time for Galen Hall," *The Tuscaloosa News,* September 15, 1986.

Florida's interim president, Robert Bryan, said in October of 1989 that Hall had admitted to making improper payments to his assistants and that UF lawyers were negotiating the terms of his resignation. Bryan then announced that the school was severing ties with its football coach— a move that saved the Gators from having further sanctions levied. As it was, they were placed on two years' probation and banned from participation in a bowl game for the 1990 season.

Hall became the second consecutive Florida coach ousted over NCAA violations. Some felt the school was being hyper sensitive in Hall's case after the 59 violations during Pell's tenure. Whether or not that was true, Florida was embarrassed—and ready to move on. Hall went 40–18–1 at UF, including a 1–2 mark against Miami.

"We made this move because the man violated his contract and committed major violations of NCAA rules," Bryan said. "We cannot allow him to coach. This is not a rogue university. But we contracted a disease in the early 1980s that my predecessor, Marshall Criser, almost broke his heart trying to cure. But I guarantee to all who are interested in the university that it will be cured."[2]

Defensive coordinator Gary Darnell was named interim coach and won his first two games, taking the Gators to 6–1. They lost four of their last five decisions, though, including a

---

[2]Associated Press, "Florida's Galen Hall Is Fired for Violations," *Lexington Dispatch,* October 6, 1989.

34–7 thumping at the hands of Washington in the Freedom Bowl. The Spurrier era was about to begin in Gainesville, when the upgrades in talent made under Hall would begin to pay dividends.

For Hall's part, the circumstances of his leaving had a lasting impact. He never landed another college head coaching post. He coached in the World League of American Football, NFL Europe, and the short-lived XFL. He worked as an assistant for the Dallas Cowboys for one season before finding a home at Penn State, his alma mater, from 2004 to '11. He served as offensive coordinator under Joe Paterno, who once proclaimed that Hall was "one heck of a coach that got screwed."[3]

As fate would have it, the Nittany Lions drew the Gators in the Outback Bowl following the 2010 season. Reporters, naturally, wanted a comment from Hall as he prepared to face his former school. If they were looking for dirt, or angst, or hard feelings, they were not going to find it.

"I love the Gators," Hall said. "They were good to me. They have great fans. Just looking forward to the challenge. Going to enjoy it. What happened there was a long time ago and I've moved on. I'm at Penn State now and I'm very happy."[4]

---

[3]Jason Lieser, "Penn State's Joe Paterno Says Former Disgraced Coach Galen Hall 'Got Screwed' by Florida Gators," *Palm Beach Post,* December 29, 2010.
[4]Ibid.

When Hall retired, he settled in Groveland, Florida, less than ninety miles from Gainesville.

The Hall File

Name: Galen Samuel Hall

Born: August 14, 1940, Altoona, Pennsylvania

Playing career: Penn State University (1959–61), Washington Redskins (1962), New York Jets (1963)

Head coaching career: University of Florida (1984–89)

25

BAD NEWS ON THE DOORSTEP: FLORIDA CANCELS SERIES

IT WAS ALMOST enough to make Sam Jankovich think twice about picking up the daily newspaper to read with his morning coffee. For it was there, in the press, that the University of Miami athletic director learned about Florida's plans to cancel its football series with the Hurricanes.

"I was shocked to learn about the Florida series through the papers," Jankovich said. "We had received no previous notice."[1]

That stunning blow came in 1990, three years after the Gators first called off games against the Hurricanes due to an expansion of their Southeastern Conference schedule. In 1987, the SEC announced it was expanding its conference

[1]Associated Press, "Florida to Drop Miami," *The Item* (Sumpter, SC), December 20, 1990.

schedule from six to seven games beginning the following year. With UF already committed to a home-and-home series with Florida State, the Gators cited a more restrictive schedule and a desire to play more games away from the South for disrupting the state's longest-running annual rivalry after forty-nine years.

There had been rumors that Florida might do the same back in 1982, before the schools signed a contract for four additional games. Miami sought a home-and-home arrangement at that time, but the Gators would only agree to two games in Gainesville, one in Miami, and another (in 1984) in Tampa.

After Florida's 1987 decision to break from the annual commitment, fans of the longtime rivalry could at least hold on to the fact it was scheduled to resume in 1992 and '93. That is, until Jankovich—along with the rest of the college football world—picked up the newspaper in December 1990 and learned otherwise.

"What Florida did was deplorable," he said at his final press conference before leaving Miami for an executive job with the New England Patriots. "I think it's unfortunate for intercollegiate athletics to have a contract in place and have to read in the paper that they're not continuing the series."[2]

This time, it was an expansion of the SEC schedule to eight games beginning in '92 that Florida pointed to as the cause.

---

[2]Associated Press, "Miami AD Departs with Shot at Gators," *Gainesville Sun,* December 22, 1990.

The Gators cited the need for six home dates to meet revenue requirements. Now that four of those dates would be filled by SEC foes and another—every other year—by Florida State, UF athletic director Jeremy Foley said the school had to retain at least some flexibility.

"Believe me, we looked at every opinion," he said. "The new (SEC) schedule really puts us in a box. It's disappointing for us, but there's no alternative."[3]

The Hurricanes faithful felt otherwise. Now that Miami had become a national power and Florida was trying to work its way back toward the top after two run-ins with the NCAA in the 1980s, UM supporters claimed Florida was afraid to play them. The sense was that Florida would rather pay Miami the $75,000 buyout clause for canceling the '92 and '93 games and schedule lesser opponents than face the Canes and risk another loss. Miami had won seven of the previous 10 games between the schools when the series was discontinued in '87.

"The world would not have come to an end if that series would have been kept alive for those two years," Jankovich said, referring to the '92 and '93 games. "Everything we've done for our football scheduling is based on the Florida and Florida State series, balancing it financially and for its attractiveness."[4]

---

[3]Associated Press, "Miami vs. Florida, Maybe Not," *The Hour* (Norwalk, CT) , December 22, 1990.

[4]Associated Press, "Miami AD Departs."

Miami was an independent at the time—not affiliated with a conference—and thus had more scheduling flexibility. Still, the Hurricanes had no sympathy for a Florida program that played both Arkansas State and Louisiana-Lafayette in 1993, a season in which the Gators were supposed to line up against their longest in-state rivals.

"The Gators can find a way," said Miami radio man Joe Zagacki. "They can take Eastern Kentucky off their schedule."

"I really don't think it had anything to do with the losing streak they had with Miami," offered longtime Florida beat writer Pat Dooley of the *Gainesville Sun*. "It really wasn't that long. I think it had more to do with the fact that playing Miami really didn't do Florida any good. I can tell you that nobody at Florida wants to have anything to do with playing Miami, and it has nothing to do with their talent or athletic ability. There's just no point in playing."

Others on both sides disagree, wanting to see the schools resume their rivalry at some kind of regular cadence, even if it isn't every year.

"I think they should make it a game that's more consistent," said Mike Pouncey, a former All-America Florida center who now plays for the Miami Dolphins. "All the fans want to see it. It would be good for both universities."

"I'm frustrated by it because it doesn't make any sense," added former Hurricanes lineman Eric Winston, now president of the NFL Players Association. "I understand there's conference politics and things like that that go along, but

Florida State and Florida have always figured it out. I think it's fun for the state to have that kind of state championship that we did there for a couple of years. I think it's great for recruits seeing teams play. I get frustrated from a football fan standpoint, because I think there's really no reason they shouldn't be playing."

Those same sentiments were on the field back in 1987, when Florida and Miami played as annual rivals for the final time. Everyone knew it would be the last meeting for a while, though no one could have predicted it was the final UF-UM game of the twentieth century.

"I'm glad we got them one more time before I leave," Florida quarterback Kerwin Bell said at the time. "I love to play against them because they're a great team."[5]

"This will mean a lot to the guys who won't get to play them again," added Miami running back Melvin Bratton before helping the Canes to a 31–4 victory in that 1987 game. "They need to taste that Gator."[6]

---

[5]Associated Press, "Miami, Florida Set for Farewell," *Reading Eagle,* September 3, 1987.

[6]Ibid.

26

SPURRIER FACES CANES AS PLAYER, COACH

BEFORE HE BECAME "The Ol' Ball Coach," Steve Spurrier experienced the Florida-Miami rivalry as a star quarterback for the Gators. He beat Miami in the first meeting, 12–10 in 1964, before dropping his final two games against the Hurricanes. One, a 21–16 loss in 1966, came in his final game in Gainesville, his last regular-season collegiate contest, and his Heisman Trophy–winning season.

If that loss stuck with him, it didn't show when Spurrier was named Florida's head coach in 1990. Or perhaps it did. Spurrier made two demands of his alma mater when taking the job—the installation of natural turf at Florida Field, and the resumption of the discontinued rivalry against Miami.

"I think most everybody that follows college football felt like our school, Florida, was afraid to play Miami," Spurrier said in the summer of 1990. "Miami was whipping us on a fairly regular basis there and Florida people felt like we didn't need to play Miami anymore. Our schedule was tough enough and we didn't need to play Miami anymore.

"If they were in the state of Michigan or something like that, I might agree. But they are right here in Florida and we are going to recruit against them. Our goal, when I got here, I said we were going to be the best in the state. If we can get better than those guys—Miami and Florida State—we are probably going to be the best in the nation. . . . They are right here in our neighborhood, and if we want to be the best we've got to play them. We are going to recruit against those guys and we need to play them.

"They may beat us for a while, but if we want to be better than them we have to play them on the field and not just hope the voters vote us ahead of them."[1]

Spurrier got his natural turf. And he almost got his wish to have the rivalry with Miami resumed. For the first year he held the UF coaching job, games were scheduled between the schools for 1992, '93, '96, and '97, with an agreement to put two more on the slate in '99 and 2000. After the 1990 season, however, when the SEC announced it was expanding its conference schedule, Florida administrators removed the Hurricanes from their future plans.

---

[1]Staff Report, "Tuesday Q&A: Steve Spurrier," *Sarasota Herald-Tribune*, July 3, 1990.

The Spurrier who had been hired disagreed with the decision. The Spurrier whose schedule was impacted by the decision accepted it, and eventually grew to support it.

"Of course, when you first get hired you want to take on everybody," Spurrier said. "But we actually got Miami on the schedule. I told [Florida AD] Bill Arnsparger, 'Coach Arns, let's get them on the schedule.' They needed games. Miami was an independent. They needed to play some big schools. So they said 'sure.' We got them on the schedule.

"Three years down the road or something like that, in 1992, the SEC added South Carolina and Arkansas and needed another conference game. So we had eight conference games, and we had Florida State. So if we started playing Miami again every year, now we got just one sort of 'choice' game where you can play somebody you almost know you're going to beat.

"Coach Arns said, 'Trust me Steve, you don't want to play all these guys.' And I looked at him and said, 'You're right.' Why should Florida have to play FSU, which, when I was there, was in the top five in the nation eleven of the twelve years we coached against them? Alabama didn't play them. Georgia didn't play them. Nobody played them but us in the conference.

"And of course [Miami] was independent most all those years, and again one of the best teams in the country. So we ended up dropping Miami and going on playing our conference schedule plus FSU."

It was a formula that worked well for the Gators, even though Miami fans did not think much of it. Between 1990 and 2001, Spurrier led Florida to six SEC championships and the school's first national title (in '96), played for another national crown ('95), and earned five SEC Coach of the Year awards as the most successful coach ever to guide the Gators. Spurrier's career record at UF was 122–27–1.

And, as fate would have it, he got his chance to coach against the Hurricanes after all. The bowl gods paired the teams in the 2001 Sugar Bowl, and New Orleans got to taste every drop of bitterness the old rivalry brought out. There was a late-night fight on Bourbon Street between members of UF and UM a few days before the game—the first meeting between the two rivals since 1987. If the venom had subsided during those years off, it was back in a big way in just one night on the town.

"They had some guys who probably talked a little bit, and we probably had some guys who talked a bit," Spurrier recalled. "So they were down there talking a little smack and I guess there was some pushing and shoving. Nobody got hurt. You know, I don't know what all happened. In my opinion both teams were at fault, certainly."

Come game time, it was the Gators absorbing most of the punishment. It was a tight contest until late, when Miami pulled away for a 37–20 triumph. In four meetings with the Hurricanes as a player or coach, it was the third consecutive loss for Spurrier.

"That was an interesting game," he said. "It was very close until they called roughing the passer on Gerard Warren when he pulled [Miami quarterback Ken] Dorsey down by his shirt tail. And that's the honest truth. He had his jersey in his fingertips and the ref said he didn't let go in time. And that was a roughing the passer [penalty] on third-and-8 or something. So they got the first down, they went down and scored and pretty much put it away. They had a heck of a team and they beat us that night."

After two seasons as head coach of the NFL's Washington Redskins, Spurrier went on to win two more SEC Coach of the Year awards at South Carolina. He remains the winningest all-time coach at two different schools—Florida and South Carolina.

"In my years at Florida, if we had a playoff system where they took the top eight teams, I think we'd have had a chance at three or four national championships. But we always had that game against FSU when they were ranked 1 or 3 or 2 or something like that, at the end of the season or prior to the SEC championship. And if we weren't playing them, we're playing in the SEC championship, and then we'd be in the national game. We'd play them, they'd knock us out, and that's what would happen. . . .We had so many rivals, and for some reason we disliked FSU more than Miami. . . . But that was back in my day."

The Spurrier File

Name: Stephen Orr Spurrier

Born: April 20, 1945, Miami Beach, Florida

Playing career: University of Florida (1963–66), San Francisco 49ers (1967–75), Tampa Bay Buccaneers (1976)

Head coaching career: Duke University (1987–89), University of Florida (1990–2001), Washington Redskins (2002–03), University of South Carolina (2005–15)

Florida's 1996 national championship

Record: 12–1

August 31	Southwestern Louisiana	Ben Hill Griffin Stadium, Gainesville, FL	W 55–21
September 7	Georgia Southern	Ben Hill Griffin Stadium, Gainesville, FL	W 62–14
September 21	at Tennessee	Neyland Stadium, Knoxville, TN	W 35–29
September 28	Kentucky	Ben Hill Griffin Stadium, Gainesville, FL	W 65–0
October 5	at Arkansas	Razorback Stadium, Fayetteville, AR	W 42–7
October 12	Louisiana State	Ben Hill Griffin Stadium, Gainesville, FL	W 56–13
October 19	Auburn	Ben Hill Griffin Stadium, Gainesville, FL	W 51–10
November 2	Georgia	Alltel Stadium, Jacksonville, FL	W 47–7

(continued on next page)

November 9	at Vanderbilt	Vanderbilt Stadium, Nashville, TN	W 28–21
November 16	South Carolina	Ben Hill Griffin Stadium, Gainesville, FL	W 52–25
November 30	at Florida State	Doak Campbell Stadium, Tallahassee, FL	L 21–24
December 7	vs. Alabama	Georgia Dome, Atlanta, GA	W 45–30
January 2, 1997	vs. Florida State	Superdome, New Orleans, LA	W 52–20

27

NOT AN OUNCE OF SWEETNESS IN THIS SUGAR

IF "THE FLOP" brought the Florida-Miami football rivalry to new levels of disdain, the events leading up to the Sugar Bowl following the 2000 season took decades of hard feelings between the schools to a place they had never been before. It was an ugly place that included fisticuffs on Bourbon Street.

There was bound to be tension when fate placed the Gators and Hurricanes in New Orleans for their first meeting since 1987. Because more than thirteen years had passed since their last meeting, it was the first chance for many fans and alumni—and certainly every player on both sides—to manifest their feelings toward the other school on an actual game day. There were also extenuating circumstances.

Miami felt cheated to be playing in the Sugar Bowl in the first place. The Hurricanes had lost an early-season game at

Washington, but had rallied to sweep their remaining nine contests while climbing to the No. 2 ranking in the country behind Oklahoma. Highlighting their winning streak was a 27–24 victory over then top-ranked Florida State in October.

When it came time for the three-year-old Bowl Championship Series system to calculate computer points, poll results, and schedule strength and determine which school would play Oklahoma for the national title, it chose one-loss Florida State instead of the one-loss Hurricanes, despite the fact the Canes had won the head-to-head matchup with the Seminoles.

"We were crushed," Miami's Andre King said. "Because how can Florida State jump us and we beat them? Head to head did not play any factor. So right away we knew the system was flawed. It messed up a chance for us to possibly win [the national] title. It was crushing."

Added Miami coach Butch Davis, "We talked a little bit to about how this could be our way to prove to everybody that we deserved to play in that national championship game, having beaten Florida State. If we could win that game in convincing fashion, we could kind of prove to everybody that they made the wrong selection. There was just a lot of emotion—a lot of motivational things. When you play Florida and when you play Florida State, it doesn't take a whole heck of a lot to get those guys fired up."

There was plenty of fire on Bourbon Street on Wednesday night, December 27, six days before kickoff. No one can say with definitive authority how it all started; firsthand accounts vary. Both coaches made efforts to downplay what some called a "brawl" between several Florida and Miami players. Neither coach, however, was there to see what happened.

What *is* known is that outside of a pizzeria on famed Bourbon Street, the mecca of New Orleans nightlife, police had to break up a late-night altercation that involved at least a dozen players from both schools, possibly as many as forty. It started with trash-talking and escalated into a physical altercation. The manager of the pizza place called it a riot, with punching, kicking, and vandalism. Punches were indeed landed, though no charges were filed.

"There are lots of fights on Bourbon Street and in the French Quarter that don't result in arrests," New Orleans Police Sergeant Paul Accardo noted. "This happens to have generated a lot of publicity because the two football teams were involved."[1]

"We were walking down Bourbon Street and they were walking down Bourbon Street, and it turned into the OK Corral or something," recalled former Florida tight end Ben Troupe. "It just kind of happened.

"The funny thing is that some of those guys were hotheads and some of them weren't, but if you had on orange, you had to fight. If you had on green and orange, you had to fight.

---

[1]Mike Penner, "Miami and Florida Are Getting Back in the Ring," *Los Angeles Times,* January 2, 2001.

It was crazy, man, but at the same time it was just a part of it. It just adds to the actual rivalry. I enjoyed it, though. I got a couple licks in. As long as I didn't get punched, I was good."

"I saw the tail end of it," Miami's King said. "People were flexing their muscles a little bit. We were dancing in the street a little bit, and then a lot of guys running back to the hotel. We had a little greeting down on Bourbon Street. Everybody was trying to audition for a Rocky movie."

"There must have been about thirty guys from each team in the middle of Bourbon Street," said Brock Berlin, a Louisiana native and true freshman quarterback for Florida at the time. "If you've seen Bourbon Street, you know how crazy it can be on any given night. But this was like the wild, wild west. People were running around everywhere and diving into buildings. It was pretty indescribable."

Oh, and then there was a football game.

While the Hurricanes were out to prove they should have been playing for the national championship, the Gators were coming off a schizophrenic finish to their season. They had been drubbed by FSU in the regular-season finale, 30–7, but rebounded to hand Auburn a 28–6 whipping in the SEC championship game. They entered the Sugar Bowl 10–2 and ranked seventh nationally, with Coach Steve Spurrier getting his first chance to coach against the Hurricanes. He had gone 1–2 against them as Florida's quarterback in the 1960s.

"I had a rude awakening to the fact that it was as big a rivalry as it was," said former UF quarterback Rex Grossman, a redshirt freshman at the time. "It started off with the fight, and started off with just being in New Orleans that week and seeing all the Miami fans and all the Florida fans.

"Those were two very good teams going at it. And looking back at the players who went on to have success from Miami, it was just unbelievable. It was like everybody was a first-rounder."

"I have a picture in my office and it has a team photo from the Sugar Bowl that year," said Davis of his last of six Miami teams. "I think we had eighty-something scholarship players, probably twenty-five walk-ons. There's somewhere in the neighborhood of about one hundred kids in the picture. And we counted it up and there were like fifty-three of those guys made it to the NFL. It was just ridiculous."

The game featured plenty of talking, taunting, hard hitting, and penalties (20 for 188 yards), but fortunately the lines crossed on Bourbon Street were not trampled in the Superdome. Both high-scoring offenses were frustrated early, particularly in the red zone. Grossman led the Gators on a seven-play, 70-yard touchdown drive on their second possession, capping it with a 23-yard TD toss to Kirk Wells, but could not get UF back into the end zone again before halftime.

Ken Dorsey then quarterbacked Miami to back-to-back scoring drives for a 10–7 lead after one quarter. The touchdown came on an 8-yard pass to tight end Jeremy Shockey. The teams traded field goals in the second quarter, sending the Hurricanes into the locker room with a slim 13–10 edge.

A Dorsey interception on the third play of the second half set up a 36-yard touchdown scamper by Earnest Graham that gave the Gators their second lead, 17–13. From there, the Hurricanes quarterback took control of the game. He found D. J. Williams and Najeh Davenport for touchdowns later in the third quarter as Miami went up by a 27–17 score. The Canes could taste victory at that point. Davenport added a short touchdown run in the fourth quarter to set the final score at 37–20.

Dorsey threw for 270 yards and three touchdowns and was voted game MVP. Graham rushed for 136 yards on just 15 carries for the Gators. In the last five minutes of the game, Miami fans began chanting "We're No. 1! We're No. 1!" It didn't turn out that way, of course. The Hurricanes left the game hoping Florida State would upset Oklahoma in the Orange Bowl and that poll voters, somehow, would turn a sympathetic eye to Miami and recognize its earlier win over FSU. It all became a moot point when Oklahoma beat the Seminoles to claim the national championship.

"We made the best of it by finishing strong and beating Florida in the Sugar Bowl," King said. "Elias Sports Bureau says the Hurricanes actually won two games that weekend—the battle on the street and then the battle in the dome. We had to toss up a few Gators. We can't walk the same street without having a little action."

28

THE RISE AND FALL OF LARRY COKER

Q: Which head coach holds the most victories, without a loss, in the Florida-Miami series?

A: Miami's Larry Coker, with a 3–0 record.

CALL IT BEING in the right place at the right time, if you will. Coker himself would not disagree with the claim he was dealt a winning hand when Butch Davis gave up the University of Miami head coaching job to take over the Cleveland Browns after the 2000 season, when the Hurricanes had fallen just short of a national title with one of the greatest collections of talent in school history. In the three NFL drafts following the 2000 campaign, twenty-six Hurricanes were selected—thirteen in the first round.

Just four of those first-round Canes left in the 2001 draft, leaving the cupboard crammed with elite talent when Coker was promoted from his offensive coordinator role. What the new boss accomplished with that talent over the next two years was unprecedented—24 consecutive wins to begin his college head coaching career and a 24–1 record in his first two years.

Coker's Hurricanes swept all 12 games in his first season. Only one was decided by a single-digit margin, a 26–24 triumph at Virginia Tech to secure their place in the national championship game, where they whipped Nebraska, 37–14, at the Rose Bowl.

The 2001 Hurricanes, who belong in any conversation about the greatest all-time teams, averaged more than 42 points per game and allowed less than 10. They embarrassed ranked teams Syracuse and Washington in back-to-back weeks by a combined score of 124–7.

"There's no doubt we were the greatest team in the history of college football, because of the things we did," said running back Najeh Davenport, who shared the backfield with future NFL stars Willis McGahee and Clinton Portis. "We played ranked teams and demolished them. We had an All-American, I believe, at every position."[1]

Added sophomore center Brett Romberg: "No college team could ever beat an NFL team. But, if you took the best players from like a five-year span who played at the University

[1]Aaron Torres, "Miami Hurricanes' Pursuit of Perfection in 2001: An Oral History," *Fox Sports*, September 17, 2014.

of Miami and assembled an NFL team, we're coming home with a Super Bowl trophy. There's no doubt about it."[2]

Those were, primarily, Coker's teams. Five players—tackle Bryant McKinnie, tight end Jeremy Shockey, and defensive backs Phillip Buchanon, Ed Reed, and Mike Rumph—were drafted in the first round after the 2001 national title. Portis went in the second.

And even with that, Coker had the Canes right back in the national title picture in 2002. They stretched their winning streak to 34 consecutive games dating back to 2000 by once again sweeping their regular-season foes. Included was a 41–16 win in Gainesville in Coker's first game against the Gators.

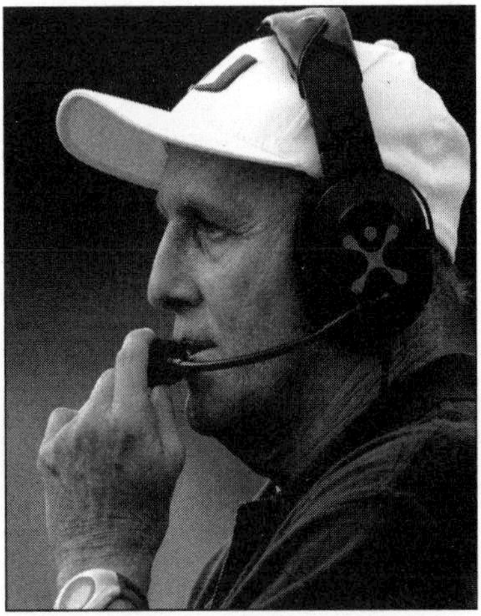

Larry Coker, shown here during a 41–16 rout of Florida in 2002, guided Miami to three wins in as many games against the Gators. Coker also steered the Hurricanes to the 2001 national championship. *AP Photo/Chris O'Meara*

"Just high-level football – the best of the best," Coker said about playing the Gators. "They had great athletes and great football players. We had great athletes and great football players. . . . That was really electric. Just a great atmosphere. It was a

[2]Ibid.

special, special game because we both were really good and had a ton of draft choices. I call a game like that 'NFL Today,' and it really was."

A one-point win against Florida State and a seven-point victory over Pittsburgh were the closest calls on the Hurricanes' march to another perfect regular season, but a championship was not to be this time, by the slimmest of margins. In one of the most exciting and controversial national title games ever played, a disputed pass interference call against Miami in the first overtime allowed Ohio State to pull out a 31–24, double-overtime upset in the Fiesta Bowl.

"That might have been the best team," Coker said, years later. "Certainly the 2001 team was a great team, but I'm not so sure the 2002 team wasn't even better, even though we didn't win the national championship. You know, that was a great run for those players.

"After the Ohio State game, I really didn't know what to say. We expected to win. You know Coach [Gregg] Popovich, with the [San Antonio] Spurs, after they lost in the NBA Finals he told them how proud he was of them, and how much he loved them. And I wish I'd have told that team how proud I was of them and how much I loved them. They were a special group and always will be."

Coker, an Oklahoma native, was a "player's coach." His greatest victory, in fact, might not have been on the field at all. It was when the Hurricanes rallied in his support when the school was looking to replace Davis. They refused to allow the job to go to an outside candidate with Coker in the building.

"There was concern about bringing someone else in and blowing up the school," recalled Coker, an offensive specialist who had coached star running backs Barry Sanders and Thurman Thomas while the offensive coordinator at Oklahoma State. "It was a great honor to get that job. And even if I hadn't gotten the job, it was a great honor to have the players step up and support you like that."

Coker's first loss, though, was the beginning of the end of Miami's dynasty as *the* elite team in college football. Four members of that 2002 team—McGahee, receiver Andre Johnson, and defensive linemen Jerome McDougle and William Joseph—were drafted in the first round. And even though six more first-rounders—safety Sean Taylor, tight end Kellen Winslow, linebackers Jonathan Vilma and D.J. Williams, and linemen Vernon Carey and Vince Wilfork—would not join the NFL until the following year, the 2003 Canes never achieved the level of success their two predecessors did. Consecutive November losses to Virginia Tech and Tennessee dropped Miami from No. 2 in the nation to No. 14, though they rallied to win their last three regular-season games and defeated Florida State in the Orange Bowl.

That 11–2 season was followed by 9–3 records in 2004 and '05, and the pressure was mounting. Talent remained in the program, but not like it did a few years earlier. The depth of great players no longer existed, and Coker was rumored to be on the hot seat. Many felt he needed to get the Hurricanes at least to a BCS bowl game in 2006 to have a shot at keeping his job, but the team went just 7–6. His '05 and '06 teams were both involved in fights, too—a scrap in the tunnel after an embarrassing Peach Bowl loss in '05 and a benches-clearing melee against Florida International in '06. Coker was fired in November.

"I don't know the direction they're going to go here," Coker said at the time. "I'm disappointed that I'm not going to be a part of it. But I just really believe some great things will happen to this program."[3]

Coker was a finalist, but not hired, for the Rice University head coaching job the following year. Two years later, he was chosen to head up a new program at the University of Texas–San Antonio. He compiled a 26–32 record with the fledgling program, including an 8–4 mark in 2012, before stepping down following the 2015 season.

The Coker File

Name: Larry Edward Coker
Born: June 23, 1948, Okemah, Oklahoma
Playing career: Northeastern State (1966–69)
Head coaching career: University of Miami (2001–06), University of Texas–San Antonio (2009–15)

---

[3]Tim Reynolds, "Miami Fires Football Coach Larry Coker," Associated Press story in the *Washington Post*, November 25, 2006.

Miami's 2001 National Championship

Record: 12–0

September 1	at Penn State	Beaver Stadium, University Park, PA	W 33–7
September 8	Rutgers	Orange Bowl, Miami, FL	W 61–0
September 27	at Pittsburgh	Heinz Field, Pittsburgh, PA	W 43–21
October 6	Troy State	Orange Bowl, Miami, FL	W 38–7
October 13	at Florida State	Doak Campbell Stadium, Tallahassee, FL	W 49–27
October 25	West Virginia	Orange Bowl, Miami, FL	W 45–3
November 3	Temple	Orange Bowl, Miami, FL	W 38–0
November 10	at Boston College	Alumni Stadium, Chestnut Hill, MA	W 18–7
November 17	Syracuse	Orange Bowl, Miami, FL	W 59–0
November 24	Washington	Orange Bowl, Miami, FL	W 65–7
December 1	at Virginia Tech	Lane Stadium, Blacksburg, VA	W 26–24
January 3, 2002	vs. Nebraska	Rose Bowl, Pasadena, CA	W 37–14

29

BERLIN SPARKS COMEBACK TO BEAT FORMER TEAM

IN 2003, MIAMI staged one of the most dramatic college football comebacks in recent memory, with Brock Berlin rallying the Hurricanes to a 38–33 victory over Florida at the Orange Bowl. The official game recap shows that the surge began with six minutes remaining in the third quarter. In the bigger picture, it actually started in 2001, when Berlin decided to transfer from UF to UM.

It was no easy decision for Berlin, a Louisiana native who was a true freshman for Steve Spurrier's Gators in 2000 and backing up fellow up-and-coming quarterback Rex Grossman in 2001. He got the chance to start the Orange Bowl to finish that '01 campaign because Grossman had violated curfew, but it was a short-term switch on the depth chart. Grossman was entrenched as the starter, and Berlin had been looking for a place he could play. He found it in Coral Gables.

"I learned a lot from Rex," Berlin shared. "It was one of those things where I wanted an opportunity to play. He was a year ahead of me—he was a redshirt freshman and I was a true freshman. When it came time to make a decision, I made the decision to go to Miami. I felt like that was going to be a better opportunity to play. Steve Spurrier was very supportive of that . . . of me going to play somewhere.

"I have nothing but positive feelings towards Florida, and towards Spurrier. I learned a lot from him, and I will always appreciate that."

Berlin was forced to sit out a year at Miami under NCAA Division I rules regarding transfers, so he was unable to impact the 2002 game between the Gators and Hurricanes. It was the first regular-season contest between the schools since 1987, and their first meeting since a Sugar Bowl clash in January 2001 that featured a fight on Bourbon Street and a Miami victory on game night.

Gainesville, hosting the Hurricanes for the first time since '86, was rocking. "The Miami people there were pretty confident that they were the better football team," Gators head coach Ron Zook recalled. "The Florida fans were probably, I don't want to say a little misled, but they had been accustomed to winning. And I think they didn't understand that the talent level wasn't the same."

The Hurricanes were coming off an undefeated national championship season in 2001 and were on their way to a run of 34 consecutive victories spanning three seasons. With Ken

Dorsey calling the signals and a roster loaded with first-round NFL talent, Miami was a juggernaut. And it showed.

Dorsey threw four touchdown passes, Willis McGahee rushed for 204 yards, and the Canes cruised to a 41–16 victory. "We heard a little bit about us being an underdog," said Miami linebacker Jonathan Vilma, "but when we looked at the film, we just felt like we were playing a better brand of football. We were tough, we were fast. They were a good team, but we just felt like we were playing a better brand of football at the time."

Added Grossman: "They were damn good. Sometimes you have to tip your cap to them. Looking back at it, they were one of the best college football teams ever. It was disappointing, to say the least."

Dorsey's graduation gave Berlin the starting job the following year, and the schedule makers gave him the Gators in his first home contest. His old teammates were coming to the Orange Bowl on September 6, with chips on their shoulders after the '02 drubbing. Though Miami had lost a host of future NFL Pro Bowl players from the '02 team, they remained among the elite teams in college football and expected no less than another convincing victory.

Berlin's former teammates had other ideas. Before the game, Gator lineman Shannon Snell said he hoped the UF defense would make his old friend's "mouth bleed."[1]

---

[1]Susan Miller Degnan, "Brock Berlin's Defining Moment as a Miami Hurricane," *Miami Herald*, September 2, 2013.

Florida came ready to play in every aspect of the game, despite fielding a team loaded with youth. The Gators played three quarterbacks—Gavin Dickey, Chris Leak, and Ingle Martin—who had started a grand total of zero road games in their careers. Their top running back, with 100 yards in the game, was freshman DeShawn Wynn.

When Wynn raced around right tackle on the first play of the second half for a 65-yard touchdown, the Gators took a stunning 26–10 lead. Minutes later, Johnny Lamar's interception of Berlin set up another UF touchdown. Florida 33, Miami 10. That was the score with six minutes to go in the third quarter.

It had all the makings of a blowout. Instead, it became a defining moment for the young man just one year removed from the opposite sideline.

"We kind of looked at each other and said, 'This is it. We need to do something now. We need to get some momentum. We need to get the ball rolling. Now's the time,'" Berlin said.

Berlin and the Canes were a different team from that point on. More accurately, they were the team they had been over the past few years. Sharp. Fast. Dominant.

An 85-yard drive to begin the comeback ended with a 26-yard touchdown toss from Berlin to Kevin Beard. A two-point conversion made it 33–18. A 62-yard pass from Berlin to Beard then put the ball on the 1-yard line, and Frank Gore ran it in just before the end of the third quarter. Berlin's 6-yard scoring strike to Ryan Moore with 11 minutes remaining in the game brought the Hurricanes to within 33–32, and every ounce of momentum was on their side. They might have gone for two points to tie, but a penalty for excessive celebration cost them that opportunity. It didn't matter, as it turned out.

"I can close my eyes and see every single thing from that game," offered Miami receiver Sinorice Moss. "It was electrifying that night in the Orange Bowl—Brock's moment to showcase to us and the rest of the world who he was as a quarterback and who we were as a team.

"We saw it in Brock's eyes. In the huddle he said we were going to do anything it took to get the victory. He was calm, but he was fired up, too."[2]

"As an offense, we just got into one of those 'zones' where it was like everything around us just slowed down," Berlin said. "It was like everybody else was going in slow motion and our offense was just doing its thing. It just started clicking. Guys started making big play after big play after big play, and you could just feel the momentum. It was the most unbelievable atmosphere I've ever been a part of to just feel that comeback. We just got to a point where we couldn't be stopped in the second half. . . . I get goosebumps just talking about it."

The Gators might have thought they stopped Berlin in the game's closing minutes, when the Miami quarterback

---

[2]Ibid.

converted a fourth-and-1 on an end run and hit the ground with painful cramps. The Canes used a timeout to keep him on the field, and the 89-yard winning drive resumed. Berlin completed an 11-yard pass to Kyle Cobia before Gore dashed into the end zone from 12 yards out. Impossibly, the Hurricanes held a 38–33 lead.

They had to hold off a final drive by the Gators, who got the ball back with 1:37 to play. But Al Marshall intercepted a Leak pass to seal the win. Berlin took a knee on the final play, then chucked the ball into the air and ran down the field doing the "Gator Chomp" with his arms—a celebration that didn't sit especially well with the Florida faithful, but one that came from spontaneous joy according to the quarterback.

"It was pure joy, and just so much pent-up emotion," Berlin said. "Gator fans had razzed me, so I looked at it as a way to razz them back. There was no hatred. I will always be a Cane, but I still have great friends from Florida—some of my closest friends in the world. I have nothing against UF."

Except one of the most memorable victories in the history of the rivalry.

30

SIXTH STRAIGHT WIN OVER FLORIDA IS A PEACH FOR CANES

CHICK-FIL-A, KNOWN FOR its "Eat More Chicken" slogan, sponsors the Peach Bowl in Atlanta. One Miami fan held up a sign at the 2004 contest that read, in green and orange, "Eat Mo' Gator."

The Hurricanes, for the sixth consecutive time in the rivalry, obliged. Their 27–10 triumph gave them their longest winning streak in the series, and it also gave quarterback Brock Berlin a unique distinction in Miami history in his final college game. The former Gator went 2–0 against his former school and 3–0 against Florida State, making sure the Hurricanes retained state bragging rights.

"There's no better feeling than beating FSU three times and Florida twice," Berlin said after the victory. "If that isn't big, I don't know what is."[1]

The previous year, in a regular-season game, Berlin had led the Hurricanes to an improbable 38–33 victory over the Gators after they trailed by 23 points late in the third quarter. This time, no comeback or fireworks were necessary. Berlin threw for a modest 171 yards, and his 20-yard touchdown pass to Ryan Moore in the third quarter effectively put the game out of Florida's reach at 24–3.

Miami did most of its damage on special teams. Kickoff return sensation Devin Hester returned a blocked field goal 78 yards for a touchdown, while Roscoe Parrish returned a punt 72 yards to the end zone. Those big plays gave UM a 17–3 halftime lead from which the Gators never recovered.

"Those guys are playmakers," Miami coach Larry Coker said. "Team speed is one thing, but to have the ability to make people miss and score touchdowns is a knack that Roscoe and Devin have."[2]

While the Hurricanes finished the season 9–3, Florida was reeling. Its head coach, Ron Zook, had been fired and Charlie Strong was making his debut as interim boss.

---

[1]Associated Press, "Hurricanes Dominate Gators Again," story appearing on ESPN.com, January 1, 2005.

[2]Ibid.

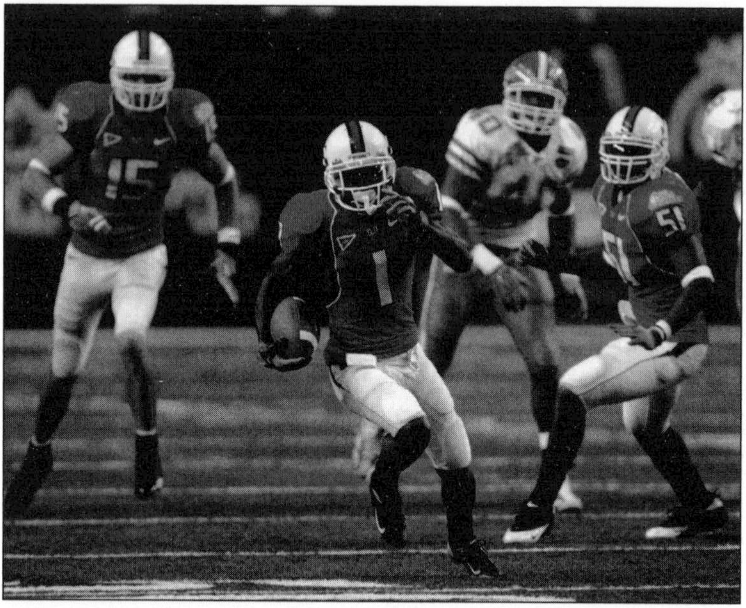

Miami's special teams were just that—special—in the 2004 Peach Bowl. Roscoe Parrish returned this punt 72 yards for a touchdown and teammate Devin Hester chipped in a 78-yard scoring return of a blocked field goal in a 27–10 drubbing of Florida. *AP Photo/John Bazemore*

Strong said the special teams breakdowns might not have taken place had Zook and his special teams coordinator not been shown the door, but acknowledged that his team was overpowered by a Miami defense that swarmed quarterback Chris Leak all night, sacking him five times and intercepting two of his passes.

"Chris was never able to get comfortable in the pocket," Strong said. "They got tons of pressure."[3]

---

[3]Ibid.

"I think our team was more mentally prepared for that game, as well as physical," Hester offered. "We out-physicaled them the whole game. It just felt like that. We wanted the game more than those guys."

It had been a topsy-turvy year for the Hurricanes. They had climbed as high as No. 3 in the AP rankings and won their first six games, but ACC losses to North Carolina, Clemson, and Virginia Tech in their final five games kept them from contending for as much as a conference championship, much less the national title that their players and fans had become accustomed to chasing.

It was a far cry from their 11–2 record of 2003, or their powerhouse performances in '01 and '02 that produced one national championship, one loss in the title game, and a 24–1 record. Still, the Peach Bowl victory secured another state championship and rounded out a dominant run of football against their bitter rivals from Gainesville.

Between 1986 and 2004, Miami had played and defeated Florida six times. They scored 197 points in those games to the Gators' 98. It remains the second-longest winning streak in the series, after Florida's seven consecutive victories in the 1970s.

"That was just a great way to end the year," Berlin said. "It was a great way to end my career. It was a great win for our team, and it was a great game for our fans. Anytime you play Florida or Florida State, there's nothing like it. It doesn't matter what the records are. Anytime you step on the field with Florida or Florida State, you know it's going to be a battle. Every down means something. There's so much on the line. It's big-time college football and I'm honored that I was a part of it."

Florida players concurred. Even with the turmoil that resulted in Zook's firing and the hiring of Urban Meyer to take over in '05, the Gators were thrilled when they heard they would play Miami in the Peach Bowl.

"It's Miami. It's not going to be hard to get our players motivated to play," Strong said. "Miami is who they really wanted to play. I'm glad it's Miami."[4]

"Before, the big thing everyone was talking about was Zook leaving," Florida linebacker Channing Crowder added before the game. "Now, it's Miami. I don't care if you play here now or played here 10 years ago, you want to beat them."[5]

Ultimately, under Meyer, Florida would end its string of futility against the Hurricanes and do just that. On this night, however, it was Berlin and Miami feasting on Gator one more time.

"It's the ultimate rivalry," Berlin said. "It's pure college football. There's just so much tradition, pride and history there. I tell you what—it's just a fun game to be involved in."

Longest Win Streaks In Series

7 – Florida (1971–77)
6 – Miami (1986–2004)
4 – Miami (1953–56), Florida (1957–60), Miami (1978–81)

---

[4]Robbie Andreu, "Gators Focused on Beating Rival Miami," *Gainesville Sun,* December 19, 2004.
[5]Ibid.

31

"URBAN RENEWAL" TAKES FLORIDA BACK TO ELITE

ONLY ONE COACH in Florida history who played the University of Miami remains undefeated against the Hurricanes. His name is Urban Meyer. Granted, Meyer only coached against the Canes once—during his 2008 national championship season. But the man has bragging rights, should he ever need them, along with a firsthand understanding of how deeply Floridians care about who wins when these two teams square off.

"It's pretty intense. I thought it would be," Meyer said of the UF-UM rivalry. "And then when we played it the one year, it's so much different than the [Florida State] rivalry because you don't really play Miami [regularly]. And there are a lot of people with some very deep-rooted feelings on both sides of the fence that think we ought to be playing all the time. So it's very intense. Obviously, Miami has got the most incredible last two decades of history of probably any football team in the country. So the word that comes to mind for me is 'intense.'"

Intense is something Meyer knows a little bit about. It's something that's been a blessing—mostly—in his coaching life, but a bit of a demon to his balance. He has been described as constantly carrying on a conversation in his head, his mind always churning, often toward a plan to win games and national championships. He has done both with uncanny success.

Many were shocked when Florida landed college football's hottest coaching commodity after the 2004 season. Notre Dame, also looking for a coach, was smitten with Meyer. Meyer had spent five years as an assistant coach with the Fighting Irish, and had once described the head position as his "dream job." He met with Notre Dame before accepting Florida's offer, but he had already decided on the Gators.

"At the University of Florida, you have everything in place to make a run at the whole thing, and that was a factor," said Meyer, who had guided Utah to 10–2 and 12–0 records in his final two years there. "I also recruited Florida for five years and I understand the type of talent that you're playing with."[1]

The Gators' final game before Meyer took over was a one-sided loss to Miami in the December 2004 Peach Bowl. UF had hired Meyer by then, but he was prepping his final

---

[1]Doug Alden, "Urban Meyer Jilts Notre Dame, Heads to Florida," Associated Press story appearing in *USA Today,* December 3, 2004.

Utah team for a Fiesta Bowl win over Pittsburgh that capped an undefeated season.

Once that game was over, it was time to put his ever-working mind to the task of building Florida back into a national power. The Gators had lost five games in each of the previous three seasons—two more than Meyer had ever experienced in a single year. Florida had the right man to right the ship.

"He's got a presence," AD Jeremy Foley said. "You walk into a room and you can tell he has a little something about him. Obviously you look at the job he's done at programs that have been less than successful [Bowling Green and Utah]. I think he does a great job with his players and has a tremendous work ethic."[2]

Meyer, an Ohio native who played defensive back at Cincinnati and two years of minor-league baseball in the Braves' system, took full advantage of his shot at big-time college football. He hit the recruiting trail hard and immediately began upgrading the talent in Gainesville. His Gators went 9–3 in his 2005 debut, including an undefeated record at "The Swamp" and an Outback Bowl victory against Iowa. Florida's only losses came at Alabama, LSU, and South Carolina (against ex-Gator Steve Spurrier).

The 2006 Gators welcomed Spurrier back to Gainesville to celebrate the tenth anniversary of their 1996 national title team—a group he coached. Then they went out and

---

[2]Ibid.

replicated the feat, going 13–1 with wins against Arkansas in the SEC championship game and Ohio State in the national title clash. UF pummeled the Buckeyes on the big stage, winning 41–14 in Glendale, Arizona.

Ohio State had entered the game undefeated, and some contended that the Gators did not deserve to be on the same field for a shot at the national crown. But following Ted Ginn Jr.'s return of the game's opening kickoff for a touchdown to give the Buckeyes a 7–0 lead, it became OSU that looked like it did not belong.

"I'd like to thank all those people" who publicly doubted and criticized the Gators before the game, Meyer said. "Our pregame speech was easy."[3]

Meyer had his critics, to be sure. Still does. During his tenure in Gainesville from 2005 to 2010, reports show that at least thirty-one of his players were arrested on various charges. The most infamous of them, tight end Aaron Hernandez, avoided his legal troubles while with the Gators adequately enough to go on to star for the New England Patriots before being convicted of murder in 2015. Hernandez was sentenced to life in prison without parole in the shooting death of his fiancée's sister's boyfriend.

Critics say Meyer recruited with little regard for whether his players could be students and good citizens first. It's a

---

[3]Associated Press, "Gators Attack: Florida Gets Title with Rout of Ohio State," ESPN.com, January 9, 2007.

dilemma for many college coaches in multiple sports, of course—familiar not just to Florida and Miami but all across the landscape. How many chances do you give young athletes who might be attending (or at least signing up for) college classes as a way of getting on the playing field, or who disregard school rules and the laws of society while being applauded for their athletic skills?

"We did make mistakes," Meyer said in 2014, referring to his time at the Florida helm. "If I look back now, the biggest mistake, I probably gave second chances to some people that maybe shouldn't [have gotten them]. But this is someone's son. I know in my soul we're doing it right, doing the best we can. Did we make mistakes? We make mistakes."[4]

Ironically, it was a soft-spoken, as-wholesome-as-they-come QB that helped Meyer win a second national title in 2008. Tim Tebow, who backed up Chris Leak during the '06 championship season and contributed one rushing touchdown and one passing score to the win over OSU, became the starter—and a national celebrity—in 2007. Tebow set several school, SEC, and national records for rushing and rushing touchdowns by a quarterback on his way to the Heisman Trophy.

The Gators went a disappointing 9–4 that year, but were loaded with talent entering 2008. With the veteran

[4]Ken Bradley, "Urban Meyer Talks About 31 Arrests at UF, Aaron Hernandez," *The Sporting News*, September 24, 2014.

Tebow under center and playmakers like receiver/kick returner Percy Harvin and linebacker Brandon Spikes demoralizing opponents, Florida showed the makings of a champion.

The early-season victory over Miami in Meyer's only meeting with the Hurricanes helped them to an impressive 3–0 start. And after a stunning 31–30 loss to Ole Miss on September 27 in Gainesville, the Gators knew their margin for error was gone. They proceeded to wipe out their remaining opponents in dominant fashion, with no game decided by less than ten points. That included a 45–15 rout of Florida State in Tallahassee, and a 24–14 win over Oklahoma in the national championship game in Miami.

The game was billed as a battle of Heisman-winning quarterbacks—Tebow (2007) vs. Sam Bradford ('08). Instead, it was a game dominated by the Florida defense. The Gators made two goal-line stands against a Sooners team that set a modern record for points in a season.

Meyer had done something no coach in Florida history had accomplished, putting two national championships in the school trophy case. Twelve consecutive wins to open the '09 season had them in the running for a third championship in the blink of an eye, but a loss to Alabama in the SEC title game cost them that chance. The toll on Meyer might have been much greater. The coach was taken to a hospital after the game with chest pains and took a leave of absence before the Sugar Bowl.

Meyer told HBO that he lost thirty-seven pounds that season, that he was battling depression and "felt like I was dying" the night after losing the SEC Championship Game. "It wasn't pretty," he said. "The toll on my body, the toll on my mind. I was physically ill."[5]

Coach Urban Meyer had precious little to be troubled about during this Florida-Miami game in 2008. The late field goal he called for set the final score at 26–3 in favor of his Gators. They went on to claim that year's national championship with a 24–14 triumph over Oklahoma in Miami. *AP Photo/Reinhold Matay*

Meyer stayed away from the game until the start of spring practice in 2010. He stuck with the team that season, but went 7–5 in the first year of the post-Tebow era and then announced his resignation, citing a desire to spend time with his family and take care of his health. He went 65–15 with two national titles in six seasons at the Florida helm and became the sixth-fastest coach to reach 100 career victories.

After a stint as an ESPN analyst, Meyer returned to coaching with Ohio State in 2012 and added another national championship in '14. He recorded his 150th career win in 2015.

---

[5]Zac Jackson, "Urban Meyer Opens Up about Trying Times in HBO Interview," *Fox Sports*, September 12, 2014.

The Meyer File

Name: Urban Frank Meyer III
Born: July 10, 1964, Toledo, Ohio
Playing career: University of Cincinnati (1984)
Head coaching career: Bowling Green University (2001–02), University of Utah (2003–04), University of Florida (2005–10), Ohio State University (2012–)

Florida's 2006 National Championship

Record: 13–1

September 2	Southern Miss	Ben Hill Griffin Stadium, Gainesville, FL	W 34–7
September 9	Central Florida	Ben Hill Griffin Stadium, Gainesville, FL	W 42–0
September 16	at Tennessee	Neyland Stadium, Knoxville, TN	W 21–20
September 23	Kentucky	Ben Hill Griffin Stadium, Gainesville, FL	W 26–7
September 30	Alabama	Ben Hill Griffin Stadium, Gainesville, FL	W 28–13
October 7	Louisiana State	Ben Hill Griffin Stadium, Gainesville, FL	W 23–10
October 14	at Auburn	Jordan-Hare Stadium, Auburn, AL	L 17–27
October 28	vs. Georgia	Alltel Stadium, Jacksonville, FL	W 21–14
November 4	at Vanderbilt	Vanderbilt Stadium, Nashville, TN	W 25–19

(continued on next page)

November 11	South Carolina	Ben Hill Griffin Stadium, Gainesville, FL	W 17–16
November 18	Western Carolina	Ben Hill Griffin Stadium, Gainesville, FL	W 62–0
November 25	at Florida State	Doak Campbell Stadium, Tallahassee, FL	W 21–14
December 2	vs. Arkansas	Georgia Dome, Atlanta, GA	W 38–28
January 8, 2007	vs. Ohio State	U. of Phoenix Stadium, Glendale, AZ	W 41–14

32

WHY THE LATE FIELD GOAL? (PART II)

ONE OF THE most talked-about games in the Florida-Miami series was the 1980 contest in which oranges were soaring toward the Canes sideline and incensed Miami coach Howard Schnellenberger fought back by running up the score with a late field goal. There was no airborne citrus when the teams did battle in Gainesville in 2008, but Florida coach Urban Meyer didn't exactly *need* the last three points of his 26–3 victory over the Hurricanes. Or did he?

"I didn't even know about it until somebody asked me about it in the press conference," Meyer said of any controversy surrounding Jonathan Phillips's 29-yard field goal in the final minute in the game. "There was zero intent [to run up the score]. The reason was we had a brand new kicker and we were going to go to Knoxville the next week [to face Tennessee]. I just kept thinking that I wanted to kick the field goal. He was a nervous kid to begin with. I wanted to see him kick the ball. That was the only reason we did that."

Miami coach Randy Shannon seemed to think there was more to it than that. "Sometimes when you do things and people see what kind of person you really are, you turn a lot of people off," Shannon said the day after the game, saying he had received numerous postgame phone calls from recruits telling him how excited they were to be coming to play for the Hurricanes. "Take from that what you want. It helped us more than you will ever know."[1]

One thing everyone agreed on was the fact the buildup to the 2008 game was intense. It was the first meeting between the schools since Miami's Peach Bowl victory over the Gators in '04 ran the Hurricanes' win streak in the series to six games.

The tide had turned over the previous few years. Meyer had come in and returned Florida to the national stage, engineering a national championship in 2006. The Gators were loaded again in '08, and Louis Murphy was not shy to let Miami know about it. Before the '08 game, the UF wide receiver said publicly that perhaps Florida, rather than Miami, should be known as "The U."

Certainly, there had been more dominant years at Miami. Coach Larry Coker had been fired after a 7–6 season in 2006,

---

[1]Michael Cunningham, "Late Gators Field Goal Leaves Shannon Miffed," *Sun Sentinel*, September 8, 2008.

and Shannon's debut in '07 produced just five wins in 12 games—the worst record for a Hurricanes team in thirty years.

Not surprisingly, Miami was a three-touchdown underdog entering the game. The atmosphere in Gainesville was celebratory even before the game. Fans in blue and orange had waited a long time to knock off the Hurricanes—almost twenty-three years to the day, to be more exact. Miami had ruled college football for much of that span, and the Gators were thrilled to be back on top.

"The magnetism, the draw, the helmets," Meyer said, referring to the Miami mystique. "The swagger that's associated with that program . . . our kids were very aware. Even [Brandon] Spikes, from North Carolina, and Percy Harvin—even the kids who weren't from Florida— there's no question. It was electric getting ready for that game. I'd say even worse than FSU just because it didn't happen very much. You know, an opportunity to beat 'The U' because there was a while there that the Florida Gators couldn't touch them."

Added Florida lineman Mike Pouncey, "I remember it being so loud you couldn't even make calls out there. The offensive line was like, 'We can't hear the QB saying the cadence.' That crowd in the Swamp is amazing every game. But when it's a game like Florida-Miami, it's unbelievable.

"Obviously, the University of Miami has won a lot of championships. They've had a lot of great players go through there. But the University of Florida has done the same thing. And that's what makes the rivalry so special."

Tim Tebow passed for two touchdowns in 2008 as Florida ended a six-game losing streak against Miami. The final score was 26–3, and a late field goal by the Gators did not sit well with many Hurricanes fans. *AP Photo/Reinhold Matay*

On this day, Miami was no match. Tim Tebow threw two touchdown passes for the Gators and the UF defense was stifling, holding the Hurricanes to 140 total yards. Robert Marve, making his first start at quarterback for the Hurricanes, passed for just 69 yards and absorbed three sacks. Florida also registered a safety on a blocked punt that rolled out of the end zone.

Murphy, the man who dubbed Florida the "New U" and who gave an inspired pregame speech to his Gator teammates about ending Miami's run of dominance in the rivalry, caught the 19-yard touchdown pass that put the game away in a 17-point fourth quarter for UF. Even the normally soft-spoken Tebow said he was thrilled to put the Gators' six-game losing streak against the Hurricanes in the rearview mirror. "I'm glad I don't have to hear about it [anymore], that's for sure," he said.[2]

---

[2]Wire Report, "Tebow, Harvin Finish Off Hurricanes with Fourth-Quarter Drives," ESPN.com, September 7, 2008.

"We were the better team, and our defense really won that game. Underline that three times," said Meyer, whose Gators went on to claim their second national championship in three years. "It was a big relief. That's one of those ones you want to enjoy, but you're so relieved you won that game that you want it to follow you around for a couple years."

Because of the on-again, off-again nature of the UF-UM rivalry, the taste of this victory did stay in Gainesville for more than a couple years. It would be five years before the schools would meet again in a football game.

"We hadn't played them in so long, and being a football player, you hear about it from everybody," Pouncey said. "You know, Miami's the best. Florida's the best. Florida State's the best. When you finally get a chance to play those teams and you beat them, you seem to get all the bragging rights, no matter how many times the team beat you previously."

Florida's 2008 National Championship

Record: 13–1

August 30	Hawaii	Ben Hill Griffin Stadium, Gainesville, FL	W 56–10
September 6	Miami (FL)	Ben Hill Griffin Stadium, Gainesville, FL	W 26–3
September 20	at Tennessee	Neyland Stadium, Knoxville, TN	W 30–6
September 27	Ole Miss	Ben Hill Griffin Stadium, Gainesville, FL	L 30–31

(continued on next page)

October 4	at Arkansas	Razorback Stadium, Fayetteville, AR	W 38–7
October 11	Louisiana State	Ben Hill Griffin Stadium, Gainesville, FL	W 51–21
October 25	Kentucky	Ben Hill Griffin Stadium, Gainesville, FL	W 63–5
November 1	vs. Georgia	Jacksonville Municipal Stadium, Jacksonville, FL	W 49–10
November 8	at Vanderbilt	Vanderbilt Stadium, Nashville, TN	W 42–14
November 15	South Carolina	Ben Hill Griffin Stadium, Gainesville, FL	W 56–6
November 22	The Citadel	Ben Hill Griffin Stadium, Gainesville, FL	W 70–19
November 29	at Florida State	Doak Campbell Stadium, Tallahassee, FL	W 45–15
December 6	vs. Alabama	Georgia Dome, Atlanta, GA	W 31–20
January 8	vs. Oklahoma	Dolphin Stadium, Miami Gardens, FL	W 24–14

33

MIAMI WINS LATEST CHAPTER IN 2013

IT WAS PERHAPS fitting that the culmination of a home-and-home series between Florida and Miami would take place five years after the opener. The second game was scheduled five years after the 2008 contest so Miami would have a marquee home date on the calendar. Because it was an odd year, the Hurricanes knew they would be playing their top two Atlantic Coast Conference rivals—Virginia Tech and Florida State—on the road. What they didn't know when they scheduled the Gators for a September 7, 2013, game is that they would soon be facing the NCAA as well.

The governing body of college sports had been looking into interactions between convicted felon Nevin Shapiro and Miami's football and basketball teams, which the Hurricanes first reported in 2009. Shapiro, a Miami booster, had been sentenced to twenty years in prison for running a $930 million Ponzi scheme. His involvement with Hurricane players reportedly included lavish parties on his yacht, at his home, and at South Florida strip clubs. The NCAA was amassing evidence that he had given improper benefits to athletes, their families, and friends by paying for meals, hotels, clothing, and gifts, among other things.

Miami had levied self-imposed bans on postseason bowl games in 2011 and '12 and had voluntarily cut down the number of scholarships offered, hoping it would help when the NCAA announced its decision. When Florida came to town in September, that day was about six weeks away, and still a dark cloud hanging over the athletic department in Coral Gables.

On the field, the Hurricanes had been looking like shadows of their former selves. Al Golden had been struggling to rebuild the talent base amid the scholarship limitations and bowl bans, and the limitations seemed to be winning. He had managed only a 13–11 record in his first two years at the helm, and a 34–6 win over Florida Atlantic in the 2013 opener did not exactly have college football powers shaking in their cleats.

Florida, meanwhile, appeared to be on the upswing. The Gators had reached the Sugar Bowl and gone 11–2 in their second year under Will Muschamp and began the '13 season ranked tenth in the AP poll. They arrived in Miami certain that they were the better team.

Statistically, they were, once the game began. Florida gained 413 yards to Miami's 212. The Gators racked up 22 first downs to the Hurricanes' 10. They enjoyed a 122–50 advantage in rushing and owned the football for nearly forty of the sixty minutes. They held Miami to a 1-for-11 success rate on third down.

Just one thing: Miami won the game, 21–16.

The difference came in the red zone. Four times, the Gators got inside the Miami 20-yard line and came away with zero points thanks to two interceptions, one fumble, and one failed fourth-down conversion. As a result, two first-quarter touchdown passes by Miami quarterback Stephen Morris gave the Hurricanes a lead they never surrendered in taking a 29–26 lead in the all-time series.

The Gators climbed within five points on a 21-yard touchdown pass from Jeff Driskel to Solomon Patton with 2:08 remaining, but Miami recovered the onside kick and stopped Florida in the late seconds.

"It's been such a hard road," Golden said, referring to the NCAA probe that was twenty-six months old at game time. "It was just a very cathartic moment. It was a great moment for our guys, all those guys that not only chose the University of Miami during this but stood there and fought."[1]

---

[1]Tim Reynolds, "Miami Upsets Florida, 21–16: No. 12 Gators Dropped By Hurricanes with Future of Rivalry in Doubt," Associated Press, story in the *Huffington Post*, September 7, 2013.

Typical of the Florida-Miami series, the fight was both physical and verbal. Not having played in five years, fans supporting both schools were at their taunting best. And it was probably worse on the field.

"We knew all week it was going to be a high trash-talking game," Morris said. "I can't tell you what was being said. It was dirty out there."[2]

"This is why you come to 'The U,'" added Tyriq McCord—whose sack of Driskel and subsequent fumble recovery with 4:32 remaining in the game set up a Duke Johnson touchdown run that made it 21–9 and essentially put the game out of reach—"to play the Florida Gators."[3]

The Hurricanes had lost 12 of their previous 14 games against teams ranked No. 12 or higher, many by wide margins. It built huge momentum for the program, which went on to win its next five games toward a 7–0 start to the season to climb to No. 7 in the poll. Three consecutive losses and the NCAA ruling put a damper on the late part of the season, but a 9–4 record was the Canes' best since '09.

The NCAA decided not to keep the Hurricanes out of any more bowl games, clearing the way for their appearance in the Russell Athletic Bowl that December. They did, however, lose nine scholarships over the next three probationary years thanks to what the NCAA decreed a "lack of institutional control."

---

[2]Ibid.

[3]Ibid.

"I want to sincerely thank our student-athletes and their families who not only stood with the University of Miami during this unprecedented challenge, but subsequently volunteered for the mission," Golden said in a statement. "They shouldered the burden, exhibited class and exemplified perseverance for Hurricanes everywhere."[4]

The troubles were of a different variety for the Gators. Florida won its next three games to climb back to No. 17 in the AP poll at the end of September. Then, the unthinkable happened. The Gators lost seven consecutive games to finish the season. One, a 26–20 loss, came at the hands of Georgia Southern.

The Gators would start the rebuilding process. With fans across the state of Florida hoping better days would include bigger and better games against the University of Miami.

---

[4]Andrea Adelson, "No Bowl Ban for Miami Hurricanes," ESPN.com, October 23, 2013.

34

WHAT'S NEXT?

THE OFFICIAL NAME of the 2019 college football season opener in Orlando, Florida, is the Camping World Kickoff. For Miami, the name of the game is Florida. For Florida, its name is Miami. And the date has been circled on each institution's calendar since the matchup was announced in April of 2016.

"We are pleased to have partnered with Florida Citrus Sports and ESPN Events to kick off the 2019 season against Miami," Florida athletic director Jeremy Foley said in renewing—at least for one game—Florida's oldest major college football rivalry. "Orlando is a great Gator city and we look forward to playing in front of our fans from all over the state of Florida and beyond."

Camping World Stadium, formerly the Citrus Bowl, was scheduled to host Florida State-Mississippi in 2016 and

Alabama-Louisville in '18. The Gators-Hurricanes game is expected to be the largest draw of the three.

"We always want to provide the fans with the ultimate experience," said Pete Derzis, senior VP for ESPN Events, "and the Gators meeting the Hurricanes in the heart of Florida certainly delivers that."

Player after player, student after student, and fan after fan declare an interest in seeing this rivalry renewed on a regular basis. "Great for the fans" is what most say to the possibility. But whether an annual game between UF and UM is great for the schools—and particularly for Florida—is a matter of great debate.

"I think it's something that they should play every year," said Brock Berlin, the quarterback who transferred from Florida to Miami and directed two victories against the Gators. "I really do. There's so much tradition there. It's such a fun game. I wish they'd figure out a way to make it happen. I hope this is not the end of it. I hope that it continues because it's an unbelievable experience as a player."

Florida holds firm in its reason for not wanting to play Miami on a regular basis—and certainly not annually, as was the case until 1987. The Gators play eight SEC schools every year, many of which are national powers, and also have an annual date with Florida State. That leaves little flexibility with the remainder of the schedule. Adding Miami every year would not only cut into that wiggle room, but would also round out a potential "murderer's row" of opponents every season.

"Every year, we play a top five team—FSU," former Florida head coach Urban Meyer said. "I do believe Miami should be on the schedule every once in a while. But you just can't play an SEC schedule, FSU, and Miami. That's just not fair. The SEC is the best conference in America, and FSU every year can be a top five team. That's OK once in a while, but you've got to be careful playing that all the time."

"Not fair," is what former coach Steve Spurrier calls the notion of facing the SEC, Florida State, and Miami year after year. He went on to suggest an alternate solution, even if it was perhaps a tongue-in-cheek notion.

"What they should do is get Miami in the SEC," Spurrier said. "But that's not going to happen. College football is not a fair sport, as we all know. It's a sport where some schools have all the advantages. Some schools naturally recruit the best players, and their schedules are naturally conducive to winning more than other schools. Florida is hurting [itself if it were to play] FSU and Miami, and eight SEC games."

Some disagree, including most everyone on the Miami side.

"It would be so awesome to bring the state together," ex-Hurricane wide receiver Andre King said. "Look at the state of Florida and the colleges that are there. Look at how we could pump that . . . if you win you win, if you lose you lose. I think they ought to find a way to get us on the schedule every two years or three years.

"We were begging to play Florida ever since we were there. But they didn't want to do it. I hope they find a way to do it."

And even some Gators got in on the quest, especially when college football adopted a playoff system in recent years. Because the top four teams at the end of the season still have a shot at the national title, former UF quarterback Rex Grossman said there's less reason for his alma mater to schedule lesser opponents in those few openings for nonconference games.

"Now that they have a playoff, I think they should play every year," Grossman said. "Figure out a way to knock one of those easier games off the schedule, because there's more margin for error, I would assume."

Florida-Miami was hardly the only heated rivalry that got eliminated or dialed back due to recent conference realignment in college football. As leagues grew, opportunities for nonconference games shrunk. And the sacrifices included some of the biggest matchups in the history of the sport—Notre Dame-Michigan, Texas-Texas A&M, Pittsburgh-Penn State, and Oklahoma-Nebraska among them.

Whatever the future holds beyond the 2019 meeting, the Florida-Miami rivalry will always be a hotly contested one—whether it's on the field, through social media channels, or on bar stools across the state. Even beyond. Those who have been a part of it tend to make sure it lives on.

"Usually, rivalry games happen long before the people who are there are involved," former Florida coach Ron Zook said. "You go back to 'The Flop.' You know, Miami people were still upset about that [when I was coaching Florida].

Rivalries are games that happen over years. Usually, it's teams that are fairly close. These guys have known each other since high school, and the majority of them are from the state of Florida. I always told our players, 'These rivalries are things that happened a long time ago. We're just honored and privileged to be a part of it.'"

APPENDIX

FLORIDA vs. MIAMI THROUGH THE YEARS

Date	Location	Winner	Score
October 15, 1938	Gainesville, FL	Miami	19–7
November 18, 1939	Miami, FL	Florida	13–0
November 16, 1940	Miami, FL	Florida	46–6
November 15, 1941	Miami, FL	Florida	14–0
November 14, 1942	Miami, FL	Miami	12–0
November 3, 1944	Miami, FL	Florida	13–0
October 19, 1945	Miami, FL	Miami	7–6
October 19, 1946	Gainesville, FL	Miami	20–13
November 22, 1947	Miami, FL	Florida	7–6
November 20, 1948	Gainesville, FL	Florida	27–13
November 18, 1949	Miami, FL	Miami	28–13
November 18, 1950	Gainesville, FL	Miami	20–14
November 17, 1951	Miami, FL	Miami	21–6

CANES VS. GATORS

Date	Location	Winner	Score
November 22, 1952	Gainesville, FL	Florida	43–6
November 28, 1953	Miami, FL	Miami	14–10
November 27, 1954	Gainesville, FL	Miami	14–0
November 26, 1955	Miami, FL	Miami	7–6
December 1, 1956	Gainesville, FL	Miami	20–7
November 30, 1957	Miami, FL	Florida	14–0
November 29, 1958	Jacksonville, FL	Florida	12–9
November 28, 1959	Jacksonville, FL	Florida	23–14
November 26, 1960	Miami, FL	Florida	18–0
December 2, 1961	Gainesville, FL	Miami	15–6
December 1, 1962	Miami, FL	Miami	17–15
November 23, 1963	Miami, FL	Florida	27–21
November 28, 1964	Gainesville, FL	Florida	12–10
November 20, 1965	Miami, FL	Miami	16–13
November 26, 1966	Gainesville, FL	Miami	21–16
December 9, 1967	Miami, FL	Miami	20–13
November 30, 1968	Gainesville, FL	Florida	14–10
November 29, 1969	Miami, FL	Florida	35–16
November 28, 1970	Gainesville, FL	Miami	14–13
November 27, 1971	Miami, FL	Florida	45–16
December 2, 1972	Gainesville, FL	Florida	17–6
November 24, 1973	Miami, FL	Florida	14–7
November 30, 1974	Gainesville, FL	Florida	31–7
November 29, 1975	Miami, FL	Florida	15–11
November 27, 1976	Orlando, FL	Florida	19–10

Date	Location	Winner	Score
November 26, 1977	Miami, FL	Florida	31–14
December 2, 1978	Gainesville, FL	Miami	22–21
December 1, 1979	Miami, FL	Miami	30–24
November 29, 1980	Gainesville, FL	Miami	31–7
September 5, 1981	Miami, FL	Miami	21–20
September 4, 1982	Gainesville, FL	Florida	17–14
September 3, 1983	Gainesville, FL	Florida	28–3
September 1, 1984	Tampa, FL	Miami	32–20
September 7, 1985	Miami, FL	Florida	35–23
September 6, 1986	Gainesville, FL	Miami	23–15
September 5, 1987	Miami, FL	Miami	31–4
January 2, 2001	New Orleans, LA (Sugar Bowl)	Miami	37–20
September 7, 2002	Gainesville, FL	Miami	41–16
September 6, 2003	Miami, FL	Miami	38–33
December 31, 2004	Atlanta, GA (Peach Bowl)	Miami	27–10
September 6, 2008	Gainesville, FL	Florida	26–3
September 7, 2013	Miami Gardens, FL	Miami	21–16
Miami leads all-time series, 29–26			

ALL-TIME COACHING RECORDS IN UF-UM GAME
(Listed in order of most victories)

Andy Gustafson, Miami	9–7
Doug Dickey, Florida	7–2
Ray Graves, Florida	5–5
Jack Harding, Miami	4–4
Bob Woodruff, Florida	4–6
Larry Coker, Miami	3–0
Jimmy Johnson, Miami	3–1
Howard Schnellenberger, Miami	3–2
Tom Lieb, Florida	3–2
Charlie Tate, Miami	3–3
Raymond Wolf, Florida	2–2
Charley Pell, Florida	2–4
Urban Meyer, Florida	1–0
Al Golden, Miami	1–0
Butch Davis, Miami	1–0
Walt Kichefski, Miami	1–0
Lou Saban, Miami	1–1
Josh Cody, Florida	1–1
Galen Hall, Florida	1–2
Steve Spurrier, Florida	0–1
Eddie Dunn, Miami	0–1
Charlie Strong, Florida	0–1
Will Muschamp, Florida	0–1
Randy Shannon, Miami	0–1

Ron Zook, Florida	0–2
Fran Curci, Miami	0–2
Pete Elliott, Miami	0–2
Carl Selmer, Miami	0–2

FLORIDA GATORS YEAR-BY-YEAR

Year	Conf.	W	L	T	Pct.	Coach	Bowl Result
2015	SEC	10	4	0	.714	Jim McElwain	Citrus Bowl-L
2014	SEC	7	5	0	.583	Will Muschamp (6–5), D.J. Durkin (1–0)	Birmingham Bowl-W
2013	SEC	4	8	0	.333	Will Muschamp	
2012	SEC	11	2	0	.846	Will Muschamp	Sugar Bowl-L
2011	SEC	7	6	0	.538	Will Muschamp	Gator Bowl-W
2010	SEC	8	5	0	.615	Urban Meyer	Outback Bowl-W
2009	SEC	13	1	0	.929	Urban Meyer	Sugar Bowl-W
2008*	SEC	13	1	0	.929	Urban Meyer	BCS Championship-W
2007	SEC	9	4	0	.692	Urban Meyer	Capital One Bowl-L
2006*	SEC	13	1	0	.929	Urban Meyer	BCS Championship-W
2005	SEC	9	3	0	.750	Urban Meyer	Outback Bowl-W
2004	SEC	7	5	0	.583	Ron Zook (7–4), Charlie Strong (0–1)	Peach Bowl-L

Year	Conf.	W	L	T	Pct.	Coach	Bowl Result
2003	SEC	8	5	0	.615	Ron Zook	Outback Bowl-L
2002	SEC	8	5	0	.615	Ron Zook	Outback Bowl-L
2001	SEC	10	2	0	.833	Steve Spurrier	Orange Bowl-W
2000	SEC	10	3	0	.769	Steve Spurrier	Sugar Bowl-L
1999	SEC	9	4	0	.692	Steve Spurrier	Citrus Bowl-L
1998	SEC	10	2	0	.833	Steve Spurrier	Orange Bowl-W
1997	SEC	10	2	0	.833	Steve Spurrier	Citrus Bowl-W
1996*	SEC	12	1	0	.923	Steve Spurrier	Sugar Bowl-W
1995	SEC	12	1	0	.923	Steve Spurrier	Fiesta Bowl-L
1994	SEC	10	2	1	.808	Steve Spurrier	Sugar Bowl-L
1993	SEC	11	2	0	.846	Steve Spurrier	Sugar Bowl-W
1992	SEC	9	4	0	.692	Steve Spurrier	Gator Bowl-W
1991	SEC	10	2	0	.833	Steve Spurrier	Sugar Bowl-L
1990	SEC	9	2	0	.818	Steve Spurrier	

Year	Conf.	W	L	T	Pct.	Coach	Bowl Result
1989	SEC	7	5	0	.583	Galen Hall (4–1), Gary Darnell (3–4)	Freedom Bowl-L
1988	SEC	7	5	0	.583	Galen Hall	All-American Bowl-W
1987	SEC	6	6	0	.500	Galen Hall	Aloha Bowl-L
1986	SEC	6	5	0	.545	Galen Hall	
1985	SEC	9	1	1	.864	Galen Hall	
1984	SEC	9	1	1	.864	Charley Pell (1-1-1), Galen Hall (8-0)	
1983	SEC	9	2	1	.792	Charley Pell	Gator Bowl-W
1982	SEC	8	4	0	.667	Charley Pell	Bluebonnet Bowl-L
1981	SEC	7	5	0	.583	Charley Pell	Peach Bowl-L
1980	SEC	8	4	0	.667	Charley Pell	TangerineBowl-W
1979	SEC	0	10	1	.045	Charley Pell	
1978	SEC	4	7	0	.364	Doug Dickey	
1977	SEC	6	4	1	.591	Doug Dickey	
1976	SEC	8	4	0	.667	Doug Dickey	Sun Bowl-L
1975	SEC	9	3	0	.750	Doug Dickey	Gator Bowl-L
1974	SEC	8	4	0	.667	Doug Dickey	Sugar Bowl-L
1973	SEC	7	5	0	.583	Doug Dickey	Tangerine Bowl-L
1972	SEC	5	5	1	.500	Doug Dickey	
1971	SEC	4	7	0	.364	Doug Dickey	
1970	SEC	7	4	0	.636	Doug Dickey	

Year	Conf.	W	L	T	Pct.	Coach	Bowl Result
1969	SEC	9	1	1	.864	Ray Graves	Gator Bowl-W
1968	SEC	6	3	1	.650	Ray Graves	
1967	SEC	6	4	0	.600	Ray Graves	
1966	SEC	9	2	0	.818	Ray Graves	Orange Bowl-W
1965	SEC	7	4	0	.636	Ray Graves	Sugar Bowl-L
1964	SEC	7	3	0	.700	Ray Graves	
1963	SEC	6	3	1	.650	Ray Graves	
1962	SEC	7	4	0	.636	Ray Graves	Gator Bowl-W
1961	SEC	4	5	1	.450	Ray Graves	
1960	SEC	9	2	0	.818	Ray Graves	Gator Bowl-W
1959	SEC	5	4	1	.550	Bob Woodruff	
1958	SEC	6	4	1	.591	Bob Woodruff	Gator Bowl-L
1957	SEC	6	2	1	.722	Bob Woodruff	
1956	SEC	6	3	1	.650	Bob Woodruff	
1955	SEC	4	6	0	.400	Bob Woodruff	
1954	SEC	5	5	0	.500	Bob Woodruff	
1953	SEC	3	5	2	.400	Bob Woodruff	
1952	SEC	8	3	0	.727	Bob Woodruff	Gator Bowl-W
1951	SEC	5	5	0	.500	Bob Woodruff	

CANES VS. GATORS

Year	Conf.	W	L	T	Pct.	Coach	Bowl Result
1950	SEC	5	5	0	.500	Bob Woodruff	
1949	SEC	4	5	1	.450	Raymond Wolf	
1948	SEC	5	5	0	.500	Raymond Wolf	
1947	SEC	4	5	1	.450	Raymond Wolf	
1946	SEC	0	9	0	.000	Raymond Wolf	
1945	SEC	4	5	1	.450	Tom Lieb	
1944	SEC	4	3	0	.571	Tom Lieb	
1942	SEC	3	7	0	.300	Tom Lieb	
1941	SEC	4	6	0	.400	Tom Lieb	
1940	SEC	5	5	0	.500	Tom Lieb	
1939	SEC	5	5	1	.500	Josh Cody	
1938	SEC	4	6	1	.409	Josh Cody	
1937	SEC	4	7	0	.364	Josh Cody	
1936	SEC	4	6	0	.400	Josh Cody	
1935	SEC	3	7	0	.300	Dutch Stanley	
1934	SEC	6	3	1	.650	Dutch Stanley	
1933	SEC	5	3	1	.611	Dutch Stanley	
1932	Southern	3	6	0	.333	Charles Bachman	

Year	Conf.	W	L	T	Pct.	Coach	Bowl Result
1931	Southern	2	6	2	.300	Charles Bachman	
1930	Southern	6	3	1	.650	Charles Bachman	
1929	Southern	8	2	0	.800	Charles Bachman	
1928	Southern	8	1	0	.889	Charles Bachman	
1927	Southern	7	3	0	.700	Tom Sebring	
1926	Southern	2	6	2	.300	Tom Sebring	
1925	Southern	8	2	0	.800	Tom Sebring	
1924	Southern	6	2	2	.700	J.A. Van Fleet	
1923	Southern	6	1	2	.778	J.A. Van Fleet	
1922	Southern	7	2	0	.778	William Kline	
1921	SIAA	6	3	2	.636	William Kline	
1920	SIAA	5	3	0	.625	William Kline	
1919	SIAA	5	3	0	.625	Al Buser	
1918	SIAA	0	1	0	.000	Al Buser	
1917	SIAA	2	4	0	.333	Al Bluser	
1916	SIAA	0	5	0	.000	Charles McCoy	
1915	SIAA	4	3	0	.571	Charles McCoy	

Year	Conf.	W	L	T	Pct.	Coach	Bowl Result
1914	SIAA	5	2	0	.714	Charles McCoy	
1913	SIAA	4	3	0	.571	G.E. Pyle	
1912	SIAA	5	2	1	.688	G.E. Pyle	
1911	Ind	5	0	1	.917	G.E. Pyle	
1910	Ind	6	1	0	.857	G.E. Pyle	
1909	Ind	6	1	1	.813	G.E. Pyle	
1908	Ind	5	2	1	.688	James Forsythe	
1907	Ind	4	1	1	.750	James Forsythe	
1906	Ind	5	3	0	625	James Forsythe	
*National Champions							

MIAMI HURRICANES YEAR-BY-YEAR

Year	Conf.	W	L	T	Pct.	Coach	Bowl Result
2015	ACC	8	5	0	.615	Larry Scott (4–2), Al Golden (4–3)	Sun Bowl-L
2014	ACC	6	7	0	.462	Al Golden	Independence Bowl-L
2013	ACC	9	4	0	.692	Al Golden	Russell Athletic Bowl-L
2012	ACC	7	5	0	.583	Al Golden	
2011	ACC	6	6	0	.500	Al Golden	
2010	ACC	7	6	0	.538	Randy Shannon (7-5), Jeff Stoutland (0-1)	Sun Bowl-L
2009	ACC	9	4	0	.692	Randy Shannon	Champs Sports Bowl-L
2008	ACC	7	6	0	.538	Randy Shannon	Emerald Bowl-L
2007	ACC	5	7	0	.417	Randy Shannon	
2006	ACC	7	6	0	.538	Larry Coker	MPC Computers Bowl-W
2005	ACC	9	3	0	.750	Larry Coker	Peach Bowl-L
2004	ACC	9	3	0	.750	Larry Coker	Peach Bowl-W
2003	Big East	11	2	0	.846	Larry Coker	Orange Bowl-W
2002	Big East	12	1	0	.923	Larry Coker	Fiesta Bowl-L
2001*	Big East	12	0	0	1.000	Larry Coker	Rose Bowl-W
2000	Big East	11	1	0	.917	Butch Davis	Sugar Bowl-W
1999	Big East	9	4	0	.692	Butch Davis	Gator Bowl-W

CANES VS. GATORS

Year	Conf.	W	L	T	Pct.	Coach	Bowl Result
1998	Big East	9	3	0	.750	Butch Davis	Micron PC Bowl-W
1997	Big East	5	6	0	.455	Butch Davis	
1996	Big East	9	3	0	.750	Butch Davis	Carquest Bowl-W
1995	Big East	8	3	0	.727	Butch Davis	
1994	Big East	10	2	0	.833	Dennis Erickson	Orange Bowl-L
1993	Big East	9	3	0	.750	Dennis Erickson	Fiesta Bowl-L
1992	Big East	11	1	0	.917	Dennis Erickson	Sugar Bowl-L
1991*	Big East	12	0	0	1.000	Dennis Erickson	Orange Bowl-W
1990	Ind	10	2	0	.833	Dennis Erickson	Cotton Bowl-W
1989*	Ind	11	1	0	.917	Dennis Erickson	Sugar Bowl-W
1988	Ind	11	1	0	.917	Jimmy Johnson	Orange Bowl-W
1987*	Ind	12	0	0	1.000	Jimmy Johnson	Orange Bowl-W
1986	Ind	11	1	0	.917	Jimmy Johnson	Fiesta Bowl-L
1985	Ind	10	2	0	.833	Jimmy Johnson	Sugar Bowl-L
1984	Ind	8	5	0	.615	Jimmy Johnson	Fiesta Bowl-L
1983*	Ind	11	1	0	.917	Howard Schnellenberger	Orange Bowl-W
1982	Ind	7	4	0	.636	Howard Schnellenberger	
1981	Ind	9	2	0	.818	Howard Schnellenberger	
1980	Ind	9	3	0	.750	Howard Schnellenberger	Peach Bowl-W

Year	Conf.	W	L	T	Pct.	Coach	Bowl Result
1979	Ind	5	6	0	.455	Howard Schnellenberger	
1978	Ind	6	5	0	.545	Lou Saban	
1977	Ind	3	8	0	.273	Lou Saban	
1976	Ind	3	8	0	.273	Carl Selmer	
1975	Ind	2	8	0	.200	Carl Selmer	
1974	Ind	6	5	0	.545	Pete Elliott	
1973	Ind	5	6	0	.455	Pete Elliott	
1972	Ind	5	6	0	.455	Fran Curci	
1971	Ind	4	7	0	.364	Fran Curci	
1970	Ind	3	8	0	.273	Charlie Tate (1-1), Walt Kichefski (2-7)	
1969	Ind	4	6	0	.400	Charlie Tate	
1968	Ind	5	5	0	.500	Charlie Tate	
1967	Ind	7	4	0	.636	Charlie Tate	Bluebonnet Bowl-L
1966	Ind	8	2	1	.773	Charlie Tate	Liberty Bowl-W
1965	Ind	5	4	1	.550	Charlie Tate	
1964	Ind	4	5	1	.450	Charlie Tate	
1963	Ind	3	7	0	.300	Andy Gustafson	
1962	Ind	7	4	0	.636	Andy Gustafson	Gotham Bowl-L
1961	Ind	7	4	0	.636	Andy Gustafson	Liberty Bowl-L
1960	Ind	6	4	0	.600	Andy Gustafson	
1959	Ind	6	4	0	.600	Andy Gustafson	
1958	Ind	2	8	0	.200	Andy Gustafson	

CANES VS. GATORS

Year	Conf.	W	L	T	Pct.	Coach	Bowl Result
1957	Ind	5	4	1	.550	Andy Gustafson	
1956	Ind	8	1	1	.850	Andy Gustafson	
1955	Ind	6	3	0	.667	Andy Gustafson	
1954	Ind	8	1	0	.889	Andy Gustafson	
1953	Ind	4	5	0	.444	Andy Gustafson	
1952	Ind	4	7	0	.364	Andy Gustafson	
1951	Ind	8	3	0	.727	Andy Gustafson	Gator Bowl-W
1950	Ind	9	1	1	.864	Andy Gustafson	Orange Bowl-L
1949	Ind	6	3	0	.667	Andy Gustafson	
1948	Ind	4	6	0	.400	Andy Gustafson	
1947	Ind	2	7	1	.250	Jack Harding	
1946	Ind	8	2	0	.800	Jack Harding	
1945	Ind	9	1	1	.864	Jack Harding	Orange Bowl-W
1944	Ind	1	7	1	.167	Eddie Dunn	
1942	SIAA	7	2	0	.778	Jack Harding	
1941	SIAA	8	2	0	.800	Jack Harding	
1940	SIAA	3	7	0	.300	Jack Harding	
1939	SIAA	5	5	0	.500	Jack Harding	
1938	SIAA	8	2	0	.800	Jack Harding	
1937	SIAA	4	4	1	.500	Jack Harding	
1936	SIAA	6	2	2	.700	Irl Tubbs	
1935	SIAA	5	3	0	.625	Irl Tubbs	
1934	SIAA	5	3	1	.688	Tom McCann	Orange Bowl-L
1933	SIAA	5	1	2	.750	Tom McCann	
1932	SIAA	4	3	1	.563	Tom McCann	
1931	SIAA	4	8	0	.333	Tom McCann	

Year	Conf.	W	L	T	Pct.	Coach	Bowl Result
1930	SIAA	3	4	1	.438	Ernest Brett	
1929	SIAA	3	2	0	.600	J. Burton Rix	
1928	Ind	4	4	1	.500	Howard Buck	
1927	Ind	3	6	1	.350	Howard Buck	
*National Champions							

INDEX

ABOUT THE AUTHOR

MARTY STRASEN'S TWENTY-YEAR career as a professional sports writer and editor spanned three national championships apiece for the Miami Hurricanes and Florida Gators. It spanned zero for his alma mater, the University of Notre Dame, though he did cover the Fighting Irish's 1988 national championship during his senior year in South Bend. After stints at *Football News/Basketball Weekly* and *The Courier* in Waterloo, Iowa, Strasen spent a decade covering sports for *The Tampa Tribune* in Tampa, Florida, contributing to coverage of both Miami and Florida football. Strasen has authored several sports books, including histories of the New York Giants and Notre Dame football teams and *Cowboys Chronicles: A Complete History of the Dallas Cowboys*. He lives in Gilroy, California, and works on the eBay campus as Global VP of Development for Triad Retail Media, an international digital agency based in Florida.